THE CUSTOMER SUCCESS FLYWHEEL

Recurring Revenue Growth:

A Practical Guide

ATMA GUNUPUDI

STARDOM BOOKS

www.StardomBooks.com

STARDOM BOOKS, LLC
112, Bordeaux Ct,
Coppell, TX 75019, USA

Copyright © 2024 by Atma Gunupudi

All rights reserved. No part of this book may be reproduced or used in any manner without written permission of the copyright owner except for the use of quotations in a book review.

FIRST EDITION JUNE 2024

STARDOM BOOKS, LLC
112 Bordeaux Ct. Coppell, TX 75019, USA

www.stardombooks.com

Stardom Books, United States
Stardom Books, India

The author and publishers have made all reasonable efforts to contact copyright holders for permission and apologize for any omissions or errors in the form of credits given. Corrections may be made to future editions.

THE CUSTOMER SUCCESS FLYWHEEL
Recurring Revenue Growth: A Practical Guide

Atma Gunupudi

p. 160
cm. 13.97 X 21.59

Category:
BUS018000: Business & Economics: Customer Relations

ISBN: 978-1-957456-49-2

I humbly dedicate this book to **Subhadra**— my mother, best friend, philosopher and guide.

CONTENTS

i	Acknowledgements	i
ii	Introduction	1
1.	Part I – SAAS and CS	3
2.	Unveiling the SaaS Revolution	5
3.	From SAAS Emergence to Customer Success Evolution	11
4.	Part II – The Customer	17
5.	Customer Obsession: The Path to Enduring Success	19
6.	The Blueprint: Customer Success Plan	25
7.	Listen, Adjust, and Thrive	37
8.	Mastering Onboarding: A Roadmap to Success	45
9.	Empowering Advocacy: Driving Growth	57
10.	Interview – How to build a Vibrant Community?	67
11.	Part III – The Team	79
12.	SaaS Success: Crafting High-Performance Teams	81

13.	Leadership Excellence for Customer Success	91
14.	The Power of the Customer Flywheel	103
15.	Mastering Metrics: Path to Success Excellence	109
16.	The Art of Driving Success Through Enablement	117
117.	Interview - Being Customer First from Day 1	125
18.	Part IV – Future	135
19.	Customer Success in Uncertain Markets	137
20.	Future of The Success Manager Role	143
	About The Author	147

ACKNOWLEDGEMENTS

- **Raviteja Dodda, Co-founder and CEO, MoEngage:**

    I would like to express my deepest appreciation to the visionary CEO, whose unwavering commitment to a customer-first approach has not only set a standard but also demonstrated the power of uniting an entire organization towards Customer Success. I am profoundly grateful for his kindness in granting me an interview, where his insights and principles on how Customer Success can foster the growth of great and successful organizations were shared. His wisdom has significantly enriched the content of this book, and his commitment to excellence continues to inspire us all. Thank you for your invaluable contribution and dedication to the cause of Customer Success.

- **Srikrishnan Ganeshan, Co-founder and CEO, Rocketlane:**

    I offer my thanks to Sri, who not only pioneered a new SAAS industry segment for the professional services realm but also recognized the paramount significance of nurturing a vibrant community as the cornerstone of his company's success. I am immensely thankful for the opportunity to interview this serial entrepreneur, during which he eloquently articulated the importance of community building. His commitment to community-first principles and his willingness to share this knowledge have undoubtedly enriched the pages of this publication, and his remarkable journey continues to inspire all who value the strength of a thriving community.

- **My Teachers:**

    This book would not have been possible without the efforts of my dedicated teachers at **Kendriya Vidyalaya Picket** and **College of Engineering - Osmania University**, who bore the responsibility for instilling in me everything I know. Their unwavering commitment to education has shaped me into a lifelong learner. I am deeply thankful for their invaluable contributions to my knowledge and growth.

- **Smith School of Business, Queen's University**

    I extend my appreciation to my MBA school and my fellow teammates - **Ali, Dheeraj, Jenny, Patrick, Stephanie,** - who imparted the invaluable skill of collaborating with individuals from diverse backgrounds and skill sets. This experience has been instrumental in building strong teams that consistently deliver outstanding results. Your guidance and camaraderie have been integral to my growth as a professional.

- **Atul Nanda, ex-SVP, Global Customer Success, Salesforce:**

    I thank Atul Nanda for being a guiding light in teaching me the profound importance of efficiently delivering customer delight while managing costs. Atul's insights have been instrumental in shaping the core principles explored in this book, and I am thankful for his wisdom and mentorship.

- **Shelly Olson, ex SVP, Adoption and Growth, Salesforce:**

    I would like to express my profound gratitude to Shelly Olson for giving me my first stretch opportunity and imparting the invaluable lesson of delivering under pressure and stepping out of my comfort zone. Shelly's mentorship and unwavering belief in my potential have played a pivotal role in shaping my journey.

- **Rob Sawyer, SVP Global Customer Support, Palo Alto Networks:**

   I am grateful to Rob for coaching me to see the bigger picture and teaching me how to take a long-term view on resources, problems, and solutions. His guidance has been instrumental in my ability to hire effectively and build and scale teams across the globe in my career.

- **My team at MoEngage:**

   I want to extend my gratitude to my team at MoEngage, with a special mention of **Raj, Prasun, and Randeep.** Your unwavering commitment to navigating the ever-evolving landscape of Customer Success, adapting to global market trends, and consistently delivering exceptional results is truly remarkable. You are the living embodiment of what it means to be champions of Customer Success. Your dedication and hard work have significantly contributed to my learnings in the field of Customer Success, and I'm grateful for your continued support and partnership.

- **Stardom Team**

   Lastly, I would like to express my heartfelt appreciation to the entire Stardom team, including Mr. Raam Anand, Rekha Krishnaprasad, and Sthitodhi Das for their unwavering commitment and meticulous efforts in bringing this book to life. As a first-time author, their unwavering support and confidence in me, my experiences, and the message I have to share have been a constant source of inspiration throughout the completion of this book.

INTRODUCTION

In "The Customer Success Flywheel," you will discover comprehensive insights into establishing and expanding customer-centric recurring revenue teams for your B2B services. Let me introduce myself— I am Atmaram Gunupudi, holding an MBA from Queen's University, Canada, and a Bachelor of Engineering from the College of Engineering at Osmania University, Hyderabad. With over two decades of experience, I have consulted on technology solutions for major enterprises worldwide, including some of the Fortune 500 companies, while also being adept at building and growing teams to drive optimal organizational results.

This book encapsulates my expertise in constructing and expanding customer-centric organizations, guaranteeing sustained revenue streams from clientele. In the first part, we shall delve into the evolution and intricacies of the Software as a Service (SaaS) paradigm. Additionally, we will explore the evolution and significance of customer success organizations, elucidating their meaning and the ideal structural configurations corresponding to various stages of your growth trajectory.

The book will be divided into two main parts. The first part focuses on building your customer success teams and scaling your organization from an outside-in perspective. It goes into the essence of creating a customer-obsessed organization. It will address questions such as: What does customer advocacy entail? How do you establish customer marketing teams? What strategies are involved in building a community? What does it mean to have a 360-degree view of the customer? How do you set up a customer flywheel and ensure unwavering commitment to your customers? How can you effectively capture customer feedback? And how do you empower your customers?

The second part will explore your customer organizations from an inside-out perspective. This entails understanding how to structure your customer success teams, defining essential competencies, managing the dynamic components, and strategically hiring leaders within these organizations. It will also cover key metrics, essential tools, and a range of best practices to effectively monitor your organization's growth. I am genuinely excited to share my insights and best practices with you.

I have also included an introductory section SaaS and the rationale behind the emergence and necessity of Customer Success Organizations, highlighting the key problems they address in the contemporary landscape. As bonus chapters towards the end, I have included discussions on the role of customer success managers during uncertain times and the evolving landscape of customer success roles.

I trust that you will find this book to be both informative and practical, serving as a manual to both construct and enhance your customer.

1

PART 1: SAAS AND CS

This introductory section lays the groundwork by providing essential context for the emergence and importance of customer success organizations.

In the chapter "Unveiling the SaaS Revolution," we embark on an enlightening exploration of Software as a Service (SaaS) and its profound impact on modern business dynamics. From its inception by Klaus Schwab to its pivotal role in shaping the Fourth Industrial Revolution, characterized by revolutionary technologies like AI and advanced robotics, we delve deep into the historical evolution of SaaS. We meticulously dissect the transition from traditional on-premises solutions to cloud-based applications, highlighting the numerous benefits of cloud computing such as scalability and simplified deployment. Yet, we also acknowledge the challenges, including customization constraints and data security concerns. By categorizing cloud services and emphasizing SaaS's potential to reshape the business landscape, we advocate for embracing its power to drive innovation and propel organizational growth.

In "From SAAS Emergence to Customer Success Evolution," we embark on a captivating journey through the historical trajectory of enterprise application businesses, setting the stage for the rise of SaaS. We illuminate the stark contrast between traditional revenue-generating teams and the disruptive impact of SaaS, which heralded the ascent of customer success teams as indispensable elements of modern business frameworks. We meticulously delineate the evolution of customer success teams through distinct stages, underscored by a shift from reactive issue resolution to proactive partnership and transformative innovation facilitation. By emphasizing the pivotal role of customer success in aligning strategies with organizational objectives, we advocate for harnessing the potential of SaaS to foster long-term success and resilience in today's dynamic marketplace.

2

UNVEILING THE SAAS REVOLUTION

Welcome aboard! Let's embark on an exciting journey into the world of Software as a Service (SaaS), the engine powering today's business landscape. Together, we will uncover the core of SaaS and its profound influence, laying the groundwork for understanding the crucial role of customer success. Join me as we unravel the mysteries of how customer success fuels recurring revenue and drives business expansion. Are you ready to dive in and explore this thrilling adventure with me?

Klaus Schwab, the founder of the world's economic forum, popularized the concept of SAAS (Software as a Service). But before getting into the history of SAAS, also known as cloud application services, it is vital to talk about the different industrial revolutions we have experienced. To summarize briefly we witnessed four industrial revolutions— The First Industrial Revolution occurred around 1784 when human beings started using machines to achieve higher results in mechanics and produce goods. In 1870, we entered the Second Industrial Revolution, where electricity was used to convert production into mass production. In 1969, we set foot into the Third Industrial Revolution, where we witnessed the rise of computers. As we speak today, we are in the Fourth Industrial Revolution, which is marked by an increase in the usage of artificial intelligence, gene editing, and advanced robotics. This phase of industrial revolutions has blurred the boundaries between physical, technical, and biological spheres.

By the Third Industrial Revolution, computers became more affordable, making them a necessity in every household. Thanks to Moore's law, computers became increasingly common, cheaper, and more powerful. By 1990, the rise of the World Wide Web (WWW) or internet disrupted businesses and made business applications widely accessible. This led to the emergence of single-tenant business software applications being available across the globe. Then, in the early 2000s, multi-tenant cloud-based applications gained popularity, providing end users with simplified access to enterprise software. This made using enterprise software as effortless as using a web-based email account.

Most enterprise solutions prior to the widespread use of cloud computing were complex on-premises applications that required deployment within the company's premises. These solutions demanded significant maintenance efforts at various levels, such as the network layer, computation layer, and infrastructure layer. In contrast, cloud-based solutions quickly gained popularity due to their numerous advantages over on-premises solutions.

Cloud computing as a concept abstracts certain maintenance tasks from end users and entrusts them to third-party service providers, resulting in simpler and easier-to-implement applications. These cloud-based applications also offer scalability, allowing businesses to effortlessly expand their operations from 50 to 5000 employees. Additionally, they eliminate the need for prolonged deployment or integration cycles, making change management much smoother.

Furthermore, cloud-based solutions provide business continuity planning by offering the ability to quickly move applications to a disaster recovery site if one of the application deployment sites experiences down time. This ensures that end user operations and use cases remain uninterrupted. In addition to their practical benefits, cloud-based solutions contribute to environmental sustainability. The concept of multi-tenancy and shared usage of resources reduces the carbon footprint, making them environmentally and economically -friendly options.

However, there are a few disadvantages of cloud computing solutions. These primarily revolve around limitations in customization and control. When utilizing a multi-tenant deployment, end users do not have complete control over the deployment process, the speed of feature releases, or the ability to customize the solution according to their specific needs.

Furthermore, cloud computing heavily relies on internet connectivity, which can pose challenges for expansion into regions with poor internet connectivity, particularly in third-world countries. Additionally, there have been significant concerns regarding data security and resiliency with Cloud based solutions, especially in industries that prioritize data security and deal with sensitive information.

Cloud services can be broadly classified into three categories. One of these categories is IAAS (Infrastructure as a Service), which offers scalable compute services for accessing and monitoring various infrastructures. IAAS eliminates the need for organizations, whether large or small, to plan, procure, and deploy hardware in advance. Prominent IAAS companies include Microsoft Azure, Rackspace, Amazon Web Services, Alibaba Elastic Compute Service, Google Cloud Platform etc.

The second category of cloud service is PAAS (Platform as a Service). Cloud-based platform services serve as building blocks, providing a framework for developers and companies to build scalable, reliable, distributed, and customized applications. These platform services enable customers to manage and maintain underlying components such as servers, data storage, and network infrastructure. Examples of PAAS include AWS Lambda, Heroku, Google App Engine, Red Hat OpenShift and more.

Finally, the third category of cloud applications is called SAAS (Software as a Service). SAAS applications are secure, scalable, and turnkey applications deployed on the cloud, accessible and utilized from anywhere. These applications offer usage-based billing to end users and abstract all layers of the application, including logic processing, compute storage, and network, making it seamless for the end user. Users simply need to log in and utilize the software for their intended purpose. Examples of SAAS applications include Salesforce, MoEngage, Rocketlane, ServiceNow, Zendesk, Dropbox etc.

SAAS applications are further classified into three categories by the National Institute of Standards and Technology (NIST), based on the infrastructure on which they are deployed. The first category is private cloud software, which is built on infrastructure exclusively provided for a single organization. While multiple consumers within the organization may utilize it, the infrastructure remains dedicated to that organization. It can be owned and managed by the organization itself or a third-party provider. The second category consists of SAAS applications deployed on the public cloud. These cloud software solutions are built on infrastructure provisioned for unrestricted use by multiple organizations simultaneously. The ownership and management of the infrastructure typically belongs to an independent entity that provides cloud services. The third category is hybrid cloud, where cloud software primarily operates on one type of infrastructure but can seamlessly switch to another during periods of high demand. This flexibility allows customers with exceptional needs at specific times to benefit from different infrastructure options. In conclusion, these three categories of SAAS applications offer organizations various options for deploying and utilizing cloud software to meet their specific requirements.

In conclusion, the evolution of Software as a Service (SaaS) has transformed businesses, offering efficiency, scalability, and accessibility. From the First Industrial Revolution to the Fourth, technology advancements have paved the way for cloud-based solutions. Cloud computing democratizes access to enterprise software, making it affordable and user-friendly. While challenges like customization limitations persist, ongoing innovations address these issues. Understanding the three primary categories of SaaS—Infrastructure as a Service (IaaS), Platform as a Service (PaaS), and Software as a Service (SaaS)—empowers organizations to tailor their approach. Embracing the power of cloud computing enables businesses to adapt to market changes and customer demands. Let's unlock the full potential of SaaS together and shape the future of business.

3

FROM SAAS EMERGENCE TO CUSTOMER SUCCESS EVOLUTION

In the previous chapter, we discussed the rise of SAAS and cloud computing. To understand customer success teams, we need to look back to the time before SAAS. Prior to the existence of SAAS companies, the enterprise application business operated linearly. Many software application providers or software consulting firms had teams that focused solely on one-time objectives. There were three main revenue generating teams: Marketing, Sales, and Professional Services:

The first team was Marketing, responsible for promoting the offered solution to the ideal customer profile, whether it was Business-to-Business (B2B) or Business-to-Consumer (B2C), with the goal of generating interest.

The second team was the sales and pre-sales team. The sales team consisted of individuals who interacted with customers to convert the generated interest into revenue by closing deals. Additionally, there were pre-sales or solutioning teams who showcased how the proposed offering could be tailored to meet the specific needs of customers.

The third team was the professional services team. The professional services team would implement the solution provided by the pre-sales and sales teams. Based on customer needs, reasonable service work order requests were made. The customers would outline their requirements, and high-level and low-level designs would be created accordingly. Months and even years of development were dedicated to these projects.

The services team would then implement the solution for the customer and hand it over to the maintenance or support team. The support team would be responsible for handling any transactional queries or issues that customers had. These support teams typically operated on Annual Maintenance Contracts or pay-as-you-go models, which required a minimal investment to ensure continued support.

This type of setup, characterized by a linear handshake, required a substantial upfront investment from customers. This investment would be allocated towards building infrastructure, acquiring machines, and establishing networking as part of the initial setup. Additionally, resources would be dedicated to developing the solutions, including considering various scenarios, building the application, and customizing it to meet customer needs over lengthy implementation cycles. This initial investment often led to the solution provider generating over 90% of their revenue from customers in the initial stages of their relationship. This also meant that it became difficult for customers to transition away from this application and migrate to a new one. As a result, there were fewer risks of customer/revenue churn.

However, as SAAS applications became more prevalent, they thoroughly disrupted the enterprise application market. Large companies started using enterprise SAAS applications because it became as easy as using websites such as www.amazon.com, Hotmail, and Gmail.

These trends were further accelerated by considerations of implementing turnkey solutions with minimal upfront payment. With the advent of SAAS enterprise solutions, a new payment model emerged where customers only paid for the scope and duration of their usage. Once they decided they were no longer getting value from the application, they had the freedom to stop using and paying. For example, if customers were dissatisfied with a solution like Salesforce Service Cloud, they could easily switch to ServiceNow and vice versa.

Consequently, the traditional one-way, handshake mechanism and setup of teams, where the marketing team positioned the product, the sales team handled sales, followed by the implementation team passing the baton to the maintenance team, and eventually forgetting about the customer, no longer worked. This was not adequate to deal with the new customer-centric model of easy exit and recurring revenue scenarios. This situation gave birth to the customer success teams. In most of the B2B SAAS companies Customer Success teams are the caretakers of the recurring revenue and play a crucial role in nurturing and retaining customers.

Different organizations require varying types of customer success teams depending on their maturity and stage of growth. Additionally, every customer success team undergoes a metamorphosis due to the changing conditions of the company. Drawing on my experience in building, scaling, and advising various organizations, I have identified four distinct stages of a customer success team's growth journey: Reactive, Proactive, Consultative, and Transformative.

The first stage is reactive customer success, commonly seen in newly launched startups that are trying to identify the right product-market fit. These companies strive to address customer needs and resolve their issues promptly. During this stage, B2B SaaS companies may experience fluctuating use cases or start with a wide range of options, aiming to identify their specific niche. Such reactive customer success organizations are defined by the way in which 90% of a CSM's duties are focused on managing customer complaints, extinguishing urgent fires, or tailoring the product to work effectively for the customers.

As companies evolve and zero in on their product-market fit, their Customer Success Teams shift into a more proactive mode. This heralds a more organized approach to customer success, shaped by insights into customers' lifecycles and usage patterns. Teams pivot to offering support, buttressed by comprehensive documentation and the tailored expertise of dedicated customer success managers. The transition from reactive to proactive is marked by an enhanced awareness of potential customer challenges and a readiness to solve them, ensuring a seamless and predictable customer experience.

In the Consultative stage, the focus shifts from product features to addressing the customer's key challenges and goals. Customer Success Managers (CSMs) take on a more strategic role, offering solutions to increase revenue, reduce costs, and improve efficiency. This stage involves deeper customer engagement and industry-specific expertise to provide personalized consultative services. CSMs proactively address customer issues with thorough documentation and engage in strategic discussions to tailor offerings that enhance customer success. Consultative maturity is characterized by the ability of the CS organization to provide solutions to customers with tangible benefits, backed by industry knowledge integrated into the team for comprehensive consultative support.

The Transformative stage is when customer success reaches its highest point, with organizations making significant changes to their customers' businesses. Here, the focus goes beyond just the product and encourages innovation, urging customers to try new strategies and find new ways to succeed. Companies like Salesforce do this with specialized teams like "ignite/Business Value Services" that help make big changes in how businesses operate. They promote ideas like digital transformation and adapt to the Fourth Industrial Revolution to redefine problem-solving, industry perspectives, and product ideas. These teams challenge customers to reconsider their strategies and expand their growth possibilities, leading to even more success.

Leaders must identify their customer success stage to adopt strategies that fuel customer satisfaction, business growth, and revenue enhancement. Today's customer success teams have evolved to become dynamic drivers of revenue expansion. They work collaboratively with marketing and sales to nurture the revenue flywheel. These teams play a vital role in strategic upselling and cross-selling, contributing significantly to a company's financial performance.

It is important for leaders to access their customer success team's position within the stages of customer success maturity, as it ensures the continuous evolution of their teams from revenue custodians to pivotal contributors to overall company success.

In summary, the evolution of Software as a Service (SaaS) and cloud computing has fundamentally transformed the enterprise application landscape. This transformation has necessitated the emergence of customer success teams as central drivers of revenue expansion and business growth. As these teams progress through stages of maturity, from reactive problem-solving to proactive partnership and transformative innovation, their role becomes increasingly vital in ensuring customer satisfaction and long-term success. By aligning customer success strategies with overarching company objectives, organizations can leverage the power of SaaS to thrive in today's dynamic marketplace.

4

PART II: THE CUSTOMER

This section delves into establishing a customer success organization, stressing customer-centric strategies for optimal outcomes. The chapter titled "Customer Obsession: The Path to Enduring Success" highlights the pivotal role of prioritizing customers, drawing insights from industry leaders like Apple, Amazon, and Nike. It advocates for integrating customer needs into all departments, fostering a company-wide culture of customer obsession, and empowering customer success teams to align with organizational goals.

Subsequently, "The Blueprint: Customer Success Plan" examines the meticulous process of understanding customers through research, tailoring approaches to address their unique needs, and devising comprehensive success plans. It emphasizes mapping stakeholders, establishing communication cadences, and leveraging customer success tools for efficient management.

Further, "Listen, Adjust, and Thrive" underscores the importance of actively seeking and valuing customer feedback. It outlines best practices for enhancing the overall customer experience and driving business growth through engagement and feedback collection mechanisms such as NPS, CES, and churn analysis.

The chapter, "Empowering Advocacy: Driving Growth," highlights the critical role of fostering customer advocacy and leveraging communities to amplify organic reach and referrals. It discusses strategies for engagement, measuring community metrics, integrating advocacy into performance evaluations, and advocating for a holistic customer success approach.

Lastly, "Mastering Onboarding: A Roadmap to Success" focuses on customer onboarding—a crucial phase introducing your company and its services. It offers insights into best practices like validating sales information, setting realistic expectations, executing robust project plans, and facilitating seamless data migration. It also stresses the importance of ongoing enablement, change management, and feedback collection for refining the customer experience and driving long-term success.

Overall, this comprehensive overview emphasizes the centrality of customer-centricity across all aspects of business operations, from culture to strategic planning and execution.

5

CUSTOMER OBSESSION: THE PATH TO ENDURING SUCCESS

After studying several companies during my career spanning twenty years, I have identified that the companies that have consistently succeeded and endured over time are those that prioritize their customers. While innovations, unique product offerings, and market positions can be easily surpassed by competitors, loyal customers remain the most valuable asset for any company. Companies that prioritize their customers, understand their needs, and focus on creating a positive impact for them are the ones that emerge as leaders in the long run. Notably, organizations such as Apple, Amazon, Costco, Harley-Davidson, and Nike are prime examples of customer-obsessed companies. These companies have built incredibly loyal customer bases which, even when presented with alternative offers at the same price, are reluctant to switch.

In this chapter, I will explore some of the key traits that customer-obsessed organizations demonstrate. First and foremost, customer-obsessed companies prioritize customers above all else. This involves ensuring that customer-facing teams, such as sales, marketing, success and service, have a strong focus on customer needs. However, it doesn't stop there. Every team within the company, including technology, back office, etc., has customers as their top priority. It is essential for every employee in the company to have a mindset that evaluates how their actions impact customers' day-to-day operations. For instance, when the engineering head plans to change a key component of the tech stack, they must consider the implications it will have on the customers and end users. Similarly, the finance team should not modify the billing tool without conducting a customer impact analysis and change management plan. They should consider questions such as the impact on end customers, their financial year, payment cycles, billing, and receivables. Even the HR team needs to exercise caution when considering changes to the timesheet tool, which allows employees to document their work before significant milestones.

One important concept that successful B2B companies understand early on is the distinction between the purchasing authority and the end users. Customer companies typically identify a specific role or individual within an organization who has the authority to make purchasing decisions. These individuals are often part of the finance, procurement, or executive team and are responsible for evaluating the financial, contractual, and value aspects of a product before deciding whether it meets the company's needs. On the other hand, the end users are the individuals who actively use the product or service on a daily basis. They are the ones who are familiar with, rely on, and interact with the tool or service in their day-to-day work. Understanding and catering to the needs of both the purchasing authority and the end users is crucial for success. Meeting the requirements of those making purchasing decisions while also ensuring that the tool or service is user-friendly and meets the daily needs of those using it will lead to greater customer satisfaction and loyalty.

THE CUSTOMER SUCCESS FLYWHEEL

An essential marker for a thriving B2B SAAS company that is customer obsessed is the existence of a highly competent and influential customer success team. A well-built customer success team serves a crucial role beyond just being representatives for customers in your company. These teams are the true guardians of your recurring revenue. They not only work to reduce churn but also play a vital role in increasing adoption and driving recurring revenue for your business. Customer success teams can act as trusted advisors for key customer stakeholders, providing direct or indirect value for your product or service. They can also offer valuable insights into leading indicators that may suggest potential customer churn. By effectively communicating these indicators to the right stakeholders and incorporating them into change management strategies, companies can enhance customer retention and transform customers into advocates.

It is essential for the customer success teams to have sufficient leverage within the organization. This includes the ability to prioritize specific products, features, or efforts within product or engineering teams. Additionally, the customer success organization should have the flexibility to help sales teams unlearn certain practices based on feedback and insights gathered from the field. To truly embed this level of customer obsession within your organization, it is important to make customer obsession part of your company's DNA. Incorporating customer success as a core value throughout the organization will foster a culture that prioritizes customer satisfaction and loyalty.

One way to ensure that customer success teams have sufficient influence within the organization and are included in the decision-making is to appropriately position the reporting hierarchy of the Customer Success organization. The most effective approach is to have the Head of Customer Success or the Chief Customer Officer report directly to the CEO. This arrangement offers two significant advantages. Firstly, it ensures that the CEO maintains a close connection with the organization's end customers, who are the most crucial stakeholders. Secondly, it grants the Customer Success organization a seat at the table alongside other important teams such as engineering, product, and sales, allowing them to effectively influence priorities.

On the other hand, if the Head of Customer Success reports into a controlling department like operations or finance, there is a risk of perceiving the Customer Success team as a cost center or a tactical team. This may lead to pressure to optimize spending or extract higher revenue from the team, which may not always align with the best interests of the end customers.

Furthermore, integrating Customer Success organizations into go-to-market teams that report to sales leadership can compromise efficiency. Conflicts of interest may arise, and the representation of the customer success team may not reach the CEO or executive group in a valid format. This makes it challenging to identify and address any undesirable sales practices or suboptimal go-to-market strategies that contribute to higher churn rates. Therefore, aligning a business-to-business software as a service company's customer success organization with the CEO is the best approach for optimal results.

In conclusion, customer obsession is a key trait of successful companies, particularly in the B2B SAAS industry. Companies that prioritize their customers, understand their needs, and focus on creating a positive impact for them are the ones that emerge as leaders in the long run. This involves ensuring that customer needs are at the forefront of every team within the organization, from sales and marketing to technology and finance. Successful B2B companies also understand the distinction between the purchasing authority and the end users, catering to the needs of both to drive customer satisfaction and loyalty. A highly competent and influential customer success team is essential in maintaining recurring revenue and increasing adoption. By prioritizing and empowering the customer success organization, companies can embed customer obsession into their DNA and foster a culture that prioritizes customer satisfaction.

Finally, positioning the customer success organization reporting hierarchy to the CEO ensures a close connection with end customers and effective influence over priorities. Ultimately, customer obsession is a critical factor in the long-term success and endurance of companies in the B2B SAAS industry.

6

THE BLUEPRINT:

CUSTOMER SUCCESS PLAN

In this chapter, we will cover the crucial aspects of understanding your customer and their success criteria. I would also like to explore the customer success plan, an invaluable tool I have extensively used throughout my career as a customer success professional. The customer success plan is a powerful resource that equips CS teams to drive the success of their customers, particularly large enterprise clients who have multiple moving parts. It serves as a comprehensive blueprint for achieving customer success.

The first step in truly knowing and serving your customers is to conduct extensive research on their industry. Understanding the dynamics of their industry is crucial. This requires understanding the various factors influencing the industry, including how government policies like data residency rules or other macroeconomic conditions impact customers' tool or service choices.

Some mature B2B SaaS companies have established industry-specific success teams to cater to specific industries. Assigning a customer success manager specializing in a particular sector enhances expertise and addresses unique customer needs. Companies can better understand their customers, build collective expertise, improve problem-solving capabilities, and gain a competitive advantage by focusing on industry verticals.

Another crucial aspect of knowing your customer is understanding their business plan and model. This involves answering important questions about their monetization plan, profitability, solvency, bottom line, and priorities. It is also crucial to identify their sustainable competitive advantage. It is important to determine how your product or service enhances or impacts their business plan, specifically their sustainable competitive advantage.

Every organization member, from CSMs to executives and support teams, must know the product or service's key value proposition. This value proposition can be categorized as cost reduction, revenue increase, or providing valuable insights via data analytics. Creating an effective "elevator pitch" for the organization ensures consistent understanding and communication of the product's value proposition.

Another crucial aspect of understanding your customer is recognizing the key stakeholders involved. There are diverse groups of stakeholders with varying personalities and levels of maturity across different spectrums of your operations. These stakeholders include buyers in enterprise organizations, SMB organizations, legal teams, information security teams, executives, and end-users. It is important to understand that there is a distinction between those making purchasing decisions and those who use the product. To succeed, your product must be appealing to both end-users and buyers.

Furthermore, it is important to have a comprehensive understanding of how these key stakeholders are interacting with different teams within your company. In a B2B SAAS setting, a customer typically has multiple touchpoints, such as the sales team, support team, customer success manager, marketing team, and professional services. The customer's executives may also connect with your company's executives and provide feedback to various teams. Throughout these interactions, customers may offer both direct and indirect feedback, which should be captured and consolidated by the customer success team in a central location.

Additionally, customer executives are pivotal stakeholders for B2B SaaS companies. They possess a comprehensive understanding of their organization and make decisions based on the value proposition you provide, which can significantly impact their organization's future. The level of interaction with these executives may vary depending on the average price of your product or service.

When researching stakeholders to understand your customers, it is crucial to comprehend their attributes. Creating personas and identifying the aspects of the product and business that are significant to each stakeholder is vital. Understanding the stakeholder journey and identifying behavioral patterns is also essential. For instance, what triggers specific actions from stakeholders? What motivates them to complete tasks on your platform? It is imperative to fully grasp and document these insights to understand what stakeholders seek from your platform.

The value proposition is at the heart of every customer research and success plan. It encompasses the intrinsic value that your product or service provides to your customers. To start, it is essential to map the key business performance indicators that hold significance for your customers and understand how your tool, platform, or services influence them. For instance, CSMs of sales automation tools should prioritize focusing on the revenue numbers of their customers. In contrast, CSMs of workforce automation tools should focus on cost savings for their customers, and so on.

To ensure the success of your tool or platform within a customer's company, it is crucial to understand their desired ideal state. As a customer success manager or leader, comprehending this perfect state should be one of your first steps. It will serve as the north star for your success plan. Starting this exercise by taking a holistic view from a high-level perspective, like from 50,000 feet, and then breaking it down to its daily implications for key customer stakeholders is highly effective.

Gathering information about the customer's mission and vision for the future is important. Understanding their methodology, unique selling points, strengths, weaknesses, opportunities, and threats is also valuable. Additionally, knowing the geographical region where customers operate and their expansion plans will provide further insights. It is also crucial to identify the milestones they plan to achieve in the next six to twelve months.

These high-level insights can be gathered from the initial discovery calls during the sales cycle and refined, tweaked, or updated based on ongoing conversations. To further understand customers' aspirations, I have found it beneficial to dedicate a portion of quarterly business reviews, steering committee meetings, and executive connections to discussing customers' ideal states.

When identifying the customer's ideal state, focusing on the areas your company's offerings can directly influence is crucial. I have observed instances where CSMs researching this area can get lost in a rabbit hole and prioritize the wrong metrics, ultimately derailing meaningful value conversations.

Once the customer's desired state has been identified, the customer success team should define the current state. This involves conducting thorough research on various metrics that hold significance for the customer and comparing them against industry benchmarks. This process marks the start of your customer success journey. In some cases, the customer may not clearly understand their current state or may not be tracking the appropriate metrics. During this initial phase, it is crucial to assist the customer in pinpointing the key metrics and determining methods to measure them accurately. Once the current state has been established, it is considered a best practice to engage in a comprehensive discussion with the customer and obtain their formal approval. This will establish a baseline for all future discussions regarding the value and return on investment the customer can anticipate achieving.

Once the current state, which serves as the starting point of your success plan, and the ideal state, representing the desired outcome, have been established, the subsequent step is to identify and thoroughly document the path that the customer success team will take to bridge the gap between these two states.

During this journey, it is crucial to continuously monitor essential metrics that will indicate your progress in the right direction. Customer experience feedback plays a pivotal role in this regard. While these metrics may not provide direct insights into the customer's path toward their ideal state, they are instrumental in assessing how customers perceive their interactions with your organization. This valuable evaluation is based on feedback from various interactions and surveys, such as verbal input during exec connections, QBRs, CSAT (Customer Satisfaction Survey), Net Promoter Scores, etc. By capturing and analyzing this feedback, you gain valuable insights into customer satisfaction and perception, enabling you to enhance their experience and direct your efforts appropriately. Different names, such as customer 360-degree view or customer health status, refer to this understanding.

In addition to understanding the customer's experience with your product, services, and teams, monitoring product and feature usage is critical to customer success planning. It is important to analyze your customer's consumption patterns and purchase behavior, comparing them to other customers' usage benchmarks. By identifying anomalies in usage patterns and deviations from typical behavior, you can mitigate risks and proactively address potential issues to ensure a seamless customer experience. These anomaly alerts are also valuable in identifying and resolving instances of excessive or insufficient usage, safeguarding the interests of your broader customer base sharing the same resources. Additionally, it's important to note that underutilization will most likely lead to revenue leakage and, in severe cases, customer churn.

The next crucial aspect of usage monitoring involves analyzing how customers engage with different features. Every Customer Success Manager (CSM) must determine if their clients must utilize certain features while neglecting others. This becomes particularly significant when implementing a multi-product GTM strategy. By tracking this data, you can not only prevent revenue loss but also gain a deeper comprehension of customer requirements across various products and features. This knowledge will enable your team to promote cross-selling opportunities effectively. Understanding which competing or related products the customer is utilizing and why can help you strengthen your position within their organization.

The billing metric is another crucial factor that must be tracked as part of your current snapshot. It is essential to be aware of how much your customers are paying you and whether there are any changes in their billing. In cases where usage-based platforms are involved, the billing metric needs to remain predictable, if not consistent, month after month, as it can vary based on customer usage. Sometimes, customers may exceed their usage limits and pay more than their initial agreement. Therefore, it is mandatory to closely monitor the billing metric and address any customer sentiment changes that arise from spikes in customer billing.

In summary, there are several aspects to consider in understanding your customers' business: their key value proposition, important stakeholders, key performance indicators for those stakeholders, the ideal state, and the current state. To effectively manage this information, investing in the right tools is crucial. Personally, I highly recommend Gainsight, one of the best customer success tools available. However, regardless of the tool you choose, ensure it allows you to stay on top of all the aspects discussed in this chapter.

Now, let's focus on the essential characteristics of a good customer success tool. Any effective customer success tool must incorporate four crucial components. The first component is data ingestion. Customers interact with your company across various touchpoints, such as sales support, marketing, and customer success. Each of these touchpoints collects valuable inputs. Suppose your success tool lacks the capability to ingest data from tools like Zendesk, which stores support cases, or Salesforce, which records customer conversations with your sales teams. In that case, you will miss out on vital information. Therefore, a good customer success tool should have the ability to accurately ingest data. It should provide APIs or plugins that enable you to consolidate data from different tools, such as sales, implementation, or professional services, into a single platform, allowing you to create a comprehensive 360-degree view of the customer.

A good customer success tool's second essential component is the ability to create and automate workflows. For example, let's say you need to establish a workflow for what a Customer Success Manager (CSM) should do 90 days before a renewal. In this case, the tool should provide the ability to create and manage such workflows or orchestrations. One tool that I highly recommend in the market is the journey orchestrator by Gainsight; however, other options are also available. The selected tool must possess automation features and provide the necessary knowledge base to empower your CSMs, making them more efficient and enabling them to automate routine tasks. This level of automation ensures smoother operations and maximizes the benefits of the tool you choose.

The third crucial component that a customer success tool must have is analytics and intelligence. With the growing buzz around artificial intelligence and machine learning, the tool needs to be capable of analyzing data from different touchpoints and identifying red flags or critical action items based on that information. Your success tool should possess the ability to analyze data and provide intelligent insights. This feature empowers you to make data-driven decisions and take proactive measures based on the intelligence gathered from the tool.

The fourth and final component of a good customer success tool is the communication module that allows the customer success team to automate important communications. This module enables you to streamline processes such as billing reminders, renewal notifications, or proactive customer engagement. Regardless of the specific requirements, the tool must have a reliable and efficient communication module. Therefore, when selecting a tool, it is imperative to consider these four components carefully. By choosing a tool that fulfills these requirements, you can benefit from enhanced automation and improved customer success management.

After discussing various aspects of understanding your customers, including their current state, desired state, and the information that should be tracked to ensure you are on the right path, let us now delve into the crux of this chapter: the success plan. Like any other plan, a success plan requires a clear end goal. Therefore, your success plan should encompass the expectations and ideal state you aim to achieve. It should also involve mapping key stakeholders from your company and the customers' organization, creating a seamless connection between them. This means outlining regular communication cadences between executives on both sides, as well as scheduling regular check-in calls with the Customer Success Manager (CSM) at predefined intervals such as weekly, monthly, or quarterly frequencies.

Once the expectations, ideal state, and stakeholder mapping are established, the next critical step is understanding your customer's current state. From there, you should develop a high-level plan that outlines key milestones and objectives to be achieved within the next three, six, and twelve months to bring customers closer to the ideal state. This section of the plan is commonly referred to as the account strategy or the plan outline.

The success plan should also include a detailed action plan in the tactical section. This should specify the assigned owners, timelines, and priorities for activities to occur in the next 30-60-90 days. It is helpful to prioritize these activities using a risk-reward (two-by-two) matrix. High-risk and high-reward tasks should precede those with low-risk and low reward. Various tools can be utilized to prioritize and track these tactical actions, but creating an action plan with clear ownership on both sides is essential.

Effective change management strategies should be vital for the success plan. This includes implementing a comprehensive training program to equip stakeholders with the necessary skills and knowledge to adapt to the new tool or platform. Additionally, a well-defined communication plan should be developed to share the new platform's value proposition and provide regular progress updates during the rollout process. Internal and external change management efforts must be carefully managed to ensure smooth transitions.

To gauge rollout progress accurately, the plan should identify relevant metrics and benchmarks to track and measure success. Sharing this data with customers fosters transparency and trust in the partnership. It is equally important to discuss any dips in metrics, addressing them promptly openly.

Moreover, aligning the impact, outcome, and key performance indicators (KPIs) mentioned previously with the plan is crucial, ensuring that the customer POC (Point of Contact) and the CSM teams are on the same page. Regularly publishing and distributing rollout milestones and KPI reports to internal and external executives and POCs will contribute to effective communication.

Integrating customer marketing into the success plan is crucial for promoting the customer's business and achieving mutual success. This includes organizing and executing targeted events and campaigns tailored to customers' needs. These initiatives can encompass impactful go-to-market strategies or compelling case studies that the customer wishes to share with their audience. Hence, it is imperative to incorporate specific customer marketing plans into the overall success plan. By doing so, we can effectively leverage various marketing channels and tactics to amplify the customer's brand presence and your platform's positive impact on them and generate favorable outcomes.

Finally, it is essential to consider the alignment of product and feature requests within the success plan. A significant portion of customers express some level of dissatisfaction with the out-of-the-box offerings in B2B SaaS platforms. However, striking a balance between fulfilling customer demands and the feasibility of implementing specific features for the broader customer base can prove to be an ongoing challenge. Each company follows its unique methodology for capturing, prioritizing, and releasing customer requests to general availability (GA). Nevertheless, maintaining an updated and comprehensive list of requested features and products, including their probability of release and tentative timelines, can be extremely beneficial. By incorporating this product and feature request alignment into the success plan, we can effectively communicate and manage customer expectations while ensuring that your company considers their needs during the product road process.

In conclusion, this chapter emphasized the importance of understanding your customers and their success criteria. It highlighted the significance of creating a customer success plan, which serves as a blueprint for customer success, particularly for large enterprise clients with complex needs. You can tailor your approach and provide targeted value by thoroughly researching the customer's industry, business plan, and key stakeholders. Additionally, implementing a robust customer success tool with data ingestion, workflow automation, analytics, and communication capabilities is crucial for effective customer success management. The success plan should outline the desired outcome, stakeholder mapping, account strategy, and a detailed action plan. Furthermore, integrating customer marketing and addressing product and feature requests in the plan can further enhance customer satisfaction and success. Overall, understanding your customers and implementing a comprehensive success plan will drive mutual success and long-term partnerships.

7

LISTEN, ADJUST, AND THRIVE

In the previous chapter, we emphasized the significance of knowing your customers and actively planning for their success. One essential aspect of achieving this success is by actively seeking and valuing your customers' feedback and input. It is crucial to establish a mechanism to listen, react, and implement changes based on their feedback. Customers can provide feedback through various channels, including direct communication, indirect signals, or specific requests. By listening to customer feedback attentively, you can identify potential churn indicators early on or leverage opportunities for up-selling or cross-selling.

Being proactive in obtaining customer feedback is important, as not all customers are naturally inclined to provide it. Your long-tail customers, disengaged customers, and those extremely busy may be less likely to offer feedback voluntarily. Therefore, it is vital to have strategies to capture feedback from these customer segments, as they can provide valuable insights regarding churn and upsell intents.

Recognizing that feedback is a critical indicator of your customers' success and neglecting to gather and act upon it can have detrimental effects.

Customer feedback can help increase revenue from your customer base or provide insight into areas where changes can be made to deliver the best possible value to your customers. Customer input can start as early as the sales process. It can be about any aspect of your company's operations, including but not limited to services, implementation, account management, customer success, tech support, product usability, feature requests, and aspects such as cost or billing.

One commonly used tool for measuring customer feedback is the Net Promoter Score (NPS). It is usually a survey-based approach to measure customer loyalty and likelihood to promote your company. It is advisable to conduct NPS surveys sparingly, as customers may become immune to these requests and stop responding. Depending on the size and age of your customer base, conducting the survey quarterly or half-yearly can be effective. During the survey, allow your customers to provide feedback at a relationship/value level rather than at a transaction level, considering it is only done once every three or six months.

I typically utilize a four-quadrant methodology for NPS surveys. The first quadrant assesses overall loyalty, while the second focuses on product-related questions regarding usability and usage. The third quadrant covers services, including implementation and customer success, and the fourth quadrant evaluates customers' perception of the value your platform generates. It is recommended to limit the number of questions to five to six and cover as many areas through them as possible. The intent is not to rush through the process but to gather meaningful feedback. Since customers provide this feedback only once every few months, it is reasonable to expect them to spend around five to ten minutes on the survey. Anything longer, you will lose customers' focus.

It is important to ensure that when sending out NPS surveys, you target customers from across the customer organization, including end users, decision-makers, and executives. This provides a comprehensive understanding of how stakeholders perceive your brand and their likelihood to recommend it. When analyzing the NPS scores, it's crucial to categorize respondents into detractors (ratings 1-6), passives (ratings 7-8), and promoters (ratings 9-10). This classification helps you understand the overall sentiment towards your brand.

Detractors are customers who are unlikely to recommend your brand and may even speak negatively about it. It's essential to address their concerns and improve their experience to mitigate potential churn or revenue shrinkage. Passive customers are somewhat satisfied but not enthusiastic enough to promote your brand actively. Engaging with them and understanding their feedback can help convert them into promoters. Promoters are your brand advocates who are highly satisfied and likely to recommend your brand to others. It's essential to nurture this group, encourage them to spread positive word-of-mouth and leverage their enthusiasm to attract new customers.

The NPS score is calculated by subtracting the percentage of detractors from the percentage of promoters. For instance, if 60% of your respondents are promoters, 20% are neutral, and 20% are detractors, your NPS score would be 40 (60% - 20%). This score is considered excellent and something to strive for, with great organizations typically ranging between 40 and 45. However, scores can vary depending on the growth stage and product maturity. By targeting a diverse range of customers and understanding their feedback through NPS surveys, you can identify areas for improvement, enhance customer satisfaction, and ultimately drive business growth.

Another metric to consider is the Customer Effort Score (CES). This metric gauges the level of effort customers require when interacting with your platform, product, or service. A lower CES score signifies a smoother and more satisfactory experience. CES is a usability indicator, especially in the initial stages of your journey towards achieving product-market fit and refining time-to-value strategies. It offers valuable insights into the efficiency of processes, the quality of customer service, and overall performance.

Businesses across diverse industries leverage CES to assess and enhance their customer experiences. Post-interaction surveys are commonly employed to measure CES. These surveys typically include a single question such as, "How easy was it to achieve your goal/objective?" or "Was your concern/issue solved by this interaction?" Respondents typically rate their experience on a Likert scale, ranging from "Strongly Disagree" to "Strongly Agree." Overall, the Customer Effort Score is a valuable tool for businesses to assess, track, and enhance customer interactions. Companies can effectively boost customer satisfaction and foster greater loyalty by striving to lower CES scores.

Various companies, especially B2B SaaS companies, also capture other types of transactional feedback. Customer satisfaction survey scores are commonly used for tactical and transactional interactions, such as tech support cases or interactions with a digital CSM who doesn't have longer-term relations with the customer. These surveys typically use a five-point scale, with five indicating very satisfied and one indicating unsatisfied.

To effectively manage customer contacts' experiences, monitoring CSAT scores and the number of negative experiences is crucial. Each company and product have specific thresholds, which can be determined through data analysis. By implementing this analysis, companies can identify when a customer contact transitions from a satisfied customer to a detractor.

Additionally, it has been observed that customers who have had negative experiences are less likely to continue using a product for an extended period. This is especially relevant for B2B SAAS companies, which often receive significant customer communication. This communication can come in various forms, such as emails, comments, or reviews. Companies can use sentiment analysis tools to assign sentiment scores to individual customers by reviewing and analyzing this feedback.

By interacting with customers and considering their feedback, companies can determine whether a customer is a promoter or detractor. This information is key to improving customer experiences and fostering customer loyalty. Furthermore, the time customers are willing to invest in a company can also offer valuable insights into their level of satisfaction and likelihood of recommending the product or service.

Moreover, companies often administer surveys at a relationship or account management level to gauge customers' willingness to maintain their contracts. These surveys, commonly called customer churn surveys, offer valuable insights into whether customers are inclined to renew their contracts. Prior to the renewal date, many companies utilize third-party discrete customer churn analysis to assess the likelihood of churn.

The most crucial feedback to capture is from customers who have decided to churn or discontinue using your services. This includes conducting thorough exit surveys. Such churn surveys offer valuable insights into the reasons behind customer churn and aid in post-churn analysis, enabling improvements for future customer relationships.

However, it is important to note that more than relying solely on reactive methods of customer feedback analysis may be required to repair relationships with existing customers. To address this, I have implemented strategic avenues for gathering input from important stakeholders, such as key executives and decision-makers, particularly in the enterprise and large customer segment.

For instance, organizing customer executive dinners or roundtables provides a platform for closed-group discussions where executives from various customers engage with our product and company executives. These gatherings offer opportunities to review our product roadmap, share product ideas, and discuss the future of our products in the industry. Such events provide a valuable opportunity for customers to share their feedback and insights regarding what is working and what is not for them and their industry. By establishing these channels for communication and collaboration, we can strengthen our relationships with customers and ensure that their voices are heard and considered in our product and service improvements.

One of the effective approaches is implementing customer advisory boards, a strategy utilized by several mature B2B SaaS companies. These boards serve as valuable tools for engaging customers as advisors in developing services, product roadmaps, and feature prioritization. When selecting customers for these advisory boards, choosing executives with extensive industry experience and a deep understanding of their specific line of work is crucial. These individuals can offer valuable insights into future industry trends and help shape our product strategies to align with successful priorities.

In addition to seeking feedback directly from customers, it is essential to actively listen and monitor any feedback shared by customers through third-party platforms. Prominent examples include tools like Google, Gartner, G2, and Forrester, where customers are motivated to share their opinions about your products and services, highlighting both positive aspects and areas for improvement. It is a good practice to allocate specific bandwidth within your customer success organizations to review and take action on feedback received through these third-party tools to enhance the overall customer experience.

Some companies in the B2B SaaS space also adopt a co-creation strategy with their customers. This approach enables collaborative feedback and the development of solutions tailored to specific verticals or industries. By closely working with customers, transformative B2B SaaS organizations create scalable solutions that address unique industry-specific challenges, leveraging customers' expertise and understanding of the problem. Implementing a co-creation strategy allows you to bring innovative and distinct solutions to the market in partnership with your customers.

Now that we have discussed various methods of capturing customer feedback, I want to share two essential best practices that will help you effectively incorporate this input into your service and product planning sessions. First and foremost, having a reliable survey or feedback tool at your disposal is crucial. SurveyMonkey is highly regarded, and Gainsight surveys are also a great option. Additionally, numerous tools on the Salesforce AppExchange can be seamlessly integrated with your CRM platform. The key is to select a tool that can automate the feedback-capturing process and is tightly integrated with your customer success tools. This ensures you have a comprehensive view of customer feedback across multiple sources at any given time. Furthermore, investing in an analytics tool that can analyze the feedback and provide insights, predictions, and intent based on the language used can greatly enhance your understanding of customer sentiments. Machine learning algorithms can also be utilized for more advanced analysis.

The second-best practice I emphasize is the importance of closing the loop with your customers. It is essential to make customers feel heard and valued. This involves documenting all feedback received, categorizing it into actionable items, and assigning tentative timelines for resolution across product and service teams in your organization. It is crucial to share this action plan with the customer. Failing to acknowledge or update customers on the progress made based on their feedback will discourage them from providing further input. Trust is a key aspect of the feedback cycle, and customers are more likely to continue giving feedback if they have confidence that their opinions are heard and acted upon. By implementing these best practices, you will enhance the overall customer experience and foster stronger relationships with your customers.

In conclusion, actively seeking and valuing customer feedback is paramount for driving success in any business endeavor. By establishing mechanisms to listen, react, and implement changes based on customer input, companies can identify areas for improvement, enhance customer satisfaction, and ultimately drive business growth. Whether through Net Promoter Scores (NPS), Customer Effort Scores (CES), customer satisfaction surveys, or other feedback channels, gathering and analyzing customer feedback offers invaluable insights into customer sentiment and preferences. Moreover, actively engaging with customers through events, advisory boards, and co-creation strategies fosters collaboration and strengthens relationships, ensuring that customer voices are heard and considered in product and service improvements. By implementing best practices such as utilizing reliable survey tools and closing the feedback loop with customers, businesses can enhance the overall customer experience and build trust and loyalty, driving long-term success and sustainable growth.

8

MASTERING ONBOARDING: A ROADMAP TO SUCCESS

The most pivotal stage within the customer lifecycle is the onboarding process. This initial interaction serves as the customer's introduction to your company and customer success organization. Depending on the maturity of your company and the complexity of your product or services, this phase may encompass aspects related to implementation, integration, enablement, or customization. During this part of a customer's lifecycle, they navigate through several steps and stages before fully utilizing their purchased product. This process includes implementation and integration, with potential customization to optimize the platform for the customer's needs. Ideally, mature SaaS organizations, especially in the B2B sector, should aim to minimize excessive customization to mitigate maintenance and upkeep costs per customer down the road. In this chapter, I strive to walk you through the various stages of customer onboarding and provide insights into best practices drawn from my experience.

The initial stage of customer onboarding involves understanding why the customer has chosen your platform or service, which is typically initiated during the sales process. However, diligent professional services/customer onboarding teams should refrain from assuming anything and must validate all information received from the sales team. This validation process often involves establishing a tri-party agreement between the sales, customers, and onboarding teams. Understanding the customer's rationale for purchasing your platform/service entails several steps. Firstly, it is crucial to grasp the customers' comprehension of their business model. What are the key drivers and objectives driving their business forward? Additionally, understanding the prevailing market conditions and industry trends impacting the customer's sector is essential.

Moreover, uncovering the primary motivation behind the customer's decision to opt for your service or product is imperative. Whether they are migrating from a competitor due to cost considerations or from an internal tool for advanced features, it is vital to delve into the reasons behind this transition. Exploring any shortcomings or limitations of their previous platform or product and understanding why they have chosen to switch to your offering is invaluable in tailoring the onboarding process to meet their specific needs.

Furthermore, it is imperative for the onboarding team to comprehend the fundamental drivers of the customer's overall business landscape. Understanding these key parameters is pivotal for aligning with the customer's success goals – specifically, identifying the essential metrics that your tool or platform can influence. This conversation and discovery process has the potential to profoundly impact the customer lifecycle throughout your company's relationship with them.

Begin by pinpointing the key metrics that your product can positively influence. If the customer isn't aware of these metrics, draw upon your experience with similar customers and industry norms to educate them on the metrics your solution can impact. While the bottom-line revenue impact is often the ultimate metric to influence, other critical parameters may include enhancing cost efficiency, boosting revenue, or streamlining operations.

Identifying these key metrics and understanding the customer's current baseline is crucial for demonstrating the future return on investment (ROI). By grasping the customer's current state and desired outcomes during implementation, you can effectively tailor your approach to meet their needs.

Therefore, it is essential to ascertain the metrics that the customer deems as critical success indicators and establish a clear understanding of their current baseline. From there, collaboratively identify where they aspire to be in terms of these metrics. This proactive approach ensures a solid foundation for driving success throughout the customer journey.

During the discovery phase, one of the most critical tasks is understanding the key contacts within your customer base. This entails identifying three major groups: the executive sponsor, the individual responsible for authorizing payments, and the decision-makers who ultimately determine the future of your product in their org. It is crucial to map out these contacts and discern whether they overlap or constitute separate groups. Additionally, it is imperative to identify the end users who regularly interact with your product on a daily basis.

Furthermore, it is necessary to differentiate between business users and technical users, as your product may cater to various teams such as sales, customer service, or marketing. You may also require support from technical teams within the customer's organization for effective and timely implementations. By comprehensively mapping out these stakeholders, you can ensure effective communication and alignment throughout the customer engagement process.

To ensure the success of your product within a customer's organization, it is essential to establish connections with both the product buyers and the technology teams involved in customer operations. This requires a thorough understanding of the key players within the customer's business and product teams. Additionally, from the outset, it is crucial to identify both promoters and detractors of your product throughout the purchase and sales cycle. While the sales team typically maps out champions, it is beneficial to independently identify supporters and detractors to gain a comprehensive understanding of your product's reception within the customer's organization.

To achieve this, conduct extensive customer research and engage in detailed analysis. Spend quality time with your customer contacts to discern their current pain points, aspirations, and personal ambitions. Understanding the motivations of key contacts at a personal level is vital, as decisions regarding tool adoption can significantly impact their careers.

Conduct market and competitor research to understand the broader context in which your customer operates. Explore their market position, growth trajectory, and challenges they face. Additionally, dig into user behavior by shadowing key contacts to gain insights into how end users interact with your product on a daily basis. This observational approach provides valuable insights into user preferences, pain points, and efficiency needs, facilitating a comprehensive understanding during the discovery phase of customer onboarding.

The second stage of customer onboarding is critical: expectation setting. While it is not ideal, it is common for sales teams to make unattainable promises during their sales cycle. In my twenty years of experience, I have witnessed instances where sales representatives deviate from standard practices, perhaps promising features or services that are not currently available but might be in the future. However, it is paramount to establish accurate expectations with the customer at the earliest.

Setting expectations involves several facets. Firstly, it is essential to thoroughly walk the customer through their service and product entitlements. This means delineating what is included in their package, contract, or variant—clarifying what is available, free of charge, and what additional features or services are available at an extra cost. This initial walkthrough lays the foundation for a transparent and mutually beneficial relationship.

The second aspect of expectation setting involves outlining realistic timelines. This includes defining what constitutes the Minimum Viable Product (MVP) and articulating the phased approach to going live. Customers need to understand the roadmap—what to expect in the initial phase, subsequent phases, and how the product or service will evolve over time. By ensuring clarity around entitlements and timelines, businesses can foster trust and alignment with their customers, setting the stage for a successful partnership.

Another essential step is to establish a steering committee composed of key stakeholders from both the customer's and your organization. This committee acts as a conduit for resolving issues and making decisions promptly. By bridging the gap between teams, the committee ensures alignment and facilitates smoother project execution. The steering committee should consist of executives empowered to make decisions that expedite the onboarding process. These meetings should be scheduled to review project progress, timelines, and product trajectory, fostering accountability and proactive problem-solving. This collaborative approach minimizes delays and ensures that both parties stay on track towards achieving the desired outcomes within the expected timeframe. Additionally, it's essential to establish a consistent cadence with your operational team, ensuring they are fully engaged in project execution on a daily basis. This ensures effective coordination and timely progress.

Reaching a mutual agreement between your organization and the customer regarding result commitments is crucial. This agreement should encompass various aspects such as time, resources, and involvement from both sides. This includes the dedication of time from the customer's product, engineering, and infrastructure teams, as well as any necessary support from departments like Learning and Development (L&D) and Human Resources (HR). Each of these contributions is integral to the success of the customer project.

The third stage, implementation, is where the technical aspects truly come into play, marking the pivotal moment where plans are put into action. This phase serves as the template for bridging any technological gaps between your team and the customer's. Depending on the nature of your product, service, or platform, this could range from minor configuration adjustments to substantial customization endeavors involving both teams.

To ensure a successful implementation, it is crucial to execute a robust project plan that engages technical resources from both sides. This involves collaboration between your engineers and those of the customer, aligning efforts to achieve the desired outcomes. Initially, the focus lies on identifying user roles and setups, which may entail establishing audit capabilities and trails, as well as involving security teams to implement proper access controls. Furthermore, it is essential to delve into aspects such as backup and business continuity strategies, ensuring that the customer's operations remain secure and resilient irrespective on the implementation progress.

When it comes to the actual integration phase involving the technical intricacies, the initial step is to meticulously plan the project. This entails mapping out a comprehensive project plan that encompasses potential risks, anticipated roadblocks, timelines, and dependencies. Once these elements are outlined, it is crucial to finalize the technical requirements through scoping and freeze them will sign offs from both sides before execution.

Adopting an agile methodology is paramount during this phase, ensuring a dynamic approach that continuously enhances the customer experience. This involves iterative cycles of development, where releases are made, feedback is gathered, and improvements are implemented accordingly. There is an abundance of expertise and literature available on crafting effective project plans within agile methodologies, providing valuable insights to guide this process efficiently.

Hence, securing a robust project plan is paramount, coupled with an extensive technical scope. The integration process unfolds through development, testing, and deployment, initially in a sandbox environment for thorough testing before transitioning to production, enabling customer utilization.

Data migration stands as a very important step, particularly when migrating from competitors' platforms or legacy systems. Preserving critical data is imperative, yet often underestimated by vendors, leading to numerous challenges. Recognizing data's significance as a valuable asset, meticulous attention to data migration complexity is essential.

Upon establishing the basic setup, the focus shifts to seamless data migration, followed by workflow automation to enhance operational efficiency. Personalized onboarding plans are critical, especially for large enterprises. While some customers prioritize swift deployment, cultivating a bespoke onboarding journey for enterprise and top-tier clients fosters long-term success. Tailored training plans, devising tailored use cases, and crafting personalized updates and project plans catering to the unique needs of each company are a few examples of areas that need personalization. By embracing this personalized approach, success leaders can cultivate enduring relationships and drive sustained success for both parties involved.

Moving to the next stage, arguably the most crucial step in the customer onboarding process, is the change management phase. Change management stands as the linchpin of successful customer onboarding. Beginning with a gradual approach is key; avoid the temptation of a big-bang rollout. Instead, initiate beta testing with a subset of customers or a limited platform release. This incremental method allows for early identification and resolution of any issues, paving the way for smoother transitions as the scope expands. Leveraging the concept of Minimum Viable Product (MVP) releases further enhances this process, focusing on delivering the most valuable and useful features to the customer first.

An essential aspect of change management is assessing the impact of your product or platform release on existing processes, workflows, and systems. Particularly crucial is understanding how it affects end-users' work, the metrics they value, and the outcomes they seek to achieve. Crafting a comprehensive support and training plan is essential to empower customers to succeed on your platform. Anticipating objections and resistance is paramount to the process. These concerns should be addressed proactively, ideally during the initial stage, utilizing insights garnered from the sales cycle. By acknowledging potential objections upfront and communicating the platform's benefits effectively, or providing a workaround where needed, you can mitigate resistance and foster smoother adoption processes.

Implement a reward mechanism like badge system to incentivize training participation and award spot bonuses as recognition to encourage learning and faster transition. Celebrate the achievements of both early adopters and proficient platform users. Cultivating and honoring champions is paramount. This entails identifying promoters and detractors as champions emerge during the customer's journey to going live. From the outset, prioritize the identification, development, and celebration of these champions. Continuously monitor adoption rates and adjust strategies accordingly. When migrating customers from competitors, devote even more resources to change management to ensure successful adoption.

This brings us to another important phase of customer onboarding— enablement. Enablement involves facilitating the customer's understanding and proficiency with your platform, product, or service. Enablement strategies encompass various components, including end-user training, targeted campaigns, and broader awareness initiatives within the customer organization. Allocating resources from your marketing budget towards running awareness campaigns is imperative, ensuring that not only end-users but also general users within the customer organization are informed. The effectiveness of these campaigns particularly depends on your potential to expand downstream. Enablement unfolds through different phases, beginning with pre-boarding activities that precede the formal onboarding process. Understanding the customer's current skill level and expertise through surveys and interviews is crucial at this stage. Identifying gaps and building plans to plug them forms the foundation.

The initial training phase encompasses comprehensive walkthroughs on setup configurations, basic use cases, and one-on-one training sessions designed to elevate general awareness among users. Emphasizing primary use cases and best practices further solidifies understanding during this basic training. Advanced product education is tailored towards crucial end-users and champions, providing in-depth training on product features, corner cases, and access to sandboxes for experimentation. This phase includes more intricate use cases, debugging skills, and problem-solving techniques, empowering users to navigate complex scenarios effectively.

Engaging users through the broader community marks the culmination of the enablement process. Building a strong community fosters collaboration and knowledge sharing, providing invaluable support to users at every level of expertise. By seamlessly integrating users into the community, you enrich their learning experience and strengthen their connection to your product or service.

In the final phase, which some people say "ever-boarding," the focus shifts to continuously engaging and empowering your users. It is vital to designate a customer enablement champion within your success team, or if you are smaller, a Customer Success Manager (CSM) can fulfill this role. Regardless, someone in your company should consistently monitor how you enable your customers, including introducing new features, product functionalities, use cases, and accommodating new customer additions.

This ongoing process involves various activities such as release reviews, facilitating testing for new features, providing sandbox access to your champions, and more. This "ever-boarding" approach helps make your existing users more adept with your tool, and new Points of Contact (POCs) can get up to speed with your tool sooner. For instance, personnel changes are inevitable, and when a champion transitions from an existing customer, new key Points of Contact (POCs) may join the customer team. It is crucial to swiftly onboard them on your product basics, advanced features, and the customer setup. Ensuring a seamless transition for these new team members contributes to the overall customer "ever-boarding" experience, deserving dedicated attention and resources.

Finally, once all aspects are in place, capturing feedback becomes paramount. Continuously gathering and acting upon feedback is essential for refining and enhancing the customer experience. One key step is conducting a post-implementation survey, which could be a Customer Satisfaction (CSAT) survey or Net Promoter Score (NPS) survey, depending on the duration. It's crucial to collect feedback from every contact involved in the process. Another action could be to schedule an exit feedback call as the onboarding phase concludes. This call, led by a senior member of the onboarding team from your company, aims to gather critical insights from key customer contacts. This provides an opportunity to receive constructive feedback from customer executives and identify areas for improvement.

Monitoring usage post-go-live is essential. Consider implementing a post-go-live hyper-care period for a couple of weeks, depending on the length of your implementation phase. Instead of abruptly ending support, ensure a gradual handover to the customer success team. Celebrating go-lives is a must for every B2B SaaS company. Allocate resources to generate case studies and PR around key launches and go-lives. This not only acknowledges the achievement but also serves as a final step of the onboarding journey.

The next stage involves handing over the customer to your Customer Success team or account management team, ensuring a smooth transition to someone in your company who will manage the customer during their steady-state phase. After publicly celebrating the go-live, ensure a warm handover to the success team for ongoing support and relationship management. It is advisable to initiate a tri-party agreement between the customer, implementation team, and the customer success team. This mirrors the agreement implemented at the beginning of the implementation phase between the sales, customer, and implementation team.

Define the post-implementation roles and responsibilities across teams to ensure continued customer interaction and support. As customers are accustomed to interacting with the professional services team during onboarding, it is crucial to clearly outline the new roles and responsibilities and gradually introduce the customer success team members. Define the escalation metrics for your support and success management teams to provide clarity to customers on whom to contact if issues arise during the steady state.

Document the handover process, focusing on any deviations from the standard implementation process. These deviations are vital for the success team to understand as they impact the customer lifecycle experience. Record any roadblocks encountered by the customer during the implementation and the solutions provided for these roadblocks. Additionally, document critical customer expectations or milestones for the next six to 12-month timeframe.

In conclusion, the customer onboarding process is a critical juncture within the customer lifecycle, serving as the gateway to a successful and enduring relationship. From understanding the customer's needs to setting clear expectations and guiding them through implementation and integration, every stage demands meticulous planning and execution. Key strategies such as establishing tri-party agreements, defining roles and responsibilities, and implementing robust change management practices are instrumental in ensuring a seamless transition for customers. Moreover, ongoing enablement and support initiatives and effective feedback mechanisms are vital for nurturing long-term customer success.

By adopting a customer-centric approach and prioritizing personalized experiences, businesses can cultivate enduring relationships, drive sustained success, and ultimately differentiate themselves in a competitive market landscape. As you navigate through the various stages of customer onboarding, please remain steadfast in your commitment to delivering value, empowering your customers, and exceeding their expectations at every turn. You can forge lasting partnerships that propel both your organizations toward continued growth.

In conclusion, the customer onboarding process is the cornerstone of building successful and enduring customer relationships. From understanding their needs to setting clear expectations, guiding them through implementation, and providing ongoing support, each stage is critical for fostering long-term success. By prioritizing personalized experiences, implementing robust change management practices, and continuously gathering feedback, businesses can differentiate themselves and drive sustained growth in today's competitive landscape. Together, let's commit to delivering value, empowering our customers, and exceeding their expectations at every step of the journey.

9

EMPOWERING ADVOCACY: DRIVING GROWTH

In this chapter, we will explore the importance of fostering customer advocacy and success. As the significance of customer success continues to surge, executives and CXOs across companies increasingly recognize customer success teams as fundamental sales drivers. Amidst the lengthening of sales cycles for acquiring new customers and the challenge of establishing trust, leveraging existing customer relationships for cross-selling and upselling often proves more feasible than acquiring entirely new customers. This dynamic is crucial for companies offering multiple products, services, or platforms, providing ample opportunities to cater to diverse customer needs and preferences.

Customer Success Marketing should be a cornerstone of any customer success organization. Drawing from my twenty years of experience, I have observed that investing in marketing to existing customers yields significantly higher returns in terms of generating additional revenue and fostering advocacy, compared to targeting prospects. Advocacy plays a pivotal role for any B2B SaaS company, primarily in establishing the credibility of your platform to prospective clients and investors. It is essential for them to grasp the sentiments of other companies regarding your platform, including their feedback, concerns, and positive experiences. This fosters trust and confidence in your offerings, laying a solid foundation for long-term relationships and growth.

Advocacy also serves as a catalyst for expanding organic reach. Even today, word-of-mouth referrals and peer reviews remain among the most credible sources of leads. Indeed, the most compelling references any customer can receive are those from their peer group at similar companies in the same industry. Recognizing that a satisfied customer can be your most effective salesperson is vital. Many buyers turn to third-party review platforms like G2, Gartner, or Forrester before making decisions. They specifically seek out referrals, reviews, or reference calls from companies of similar size and industry using your products or services. Customers closely scrutinize your company's ratings and feedback from existing clients on these platforms. Therefore, advocacy becomes indispensable for your sales cycles and growth journey. While promoters play a crucial role in your upsell strategy, it is important to acknowledge that not all customer interactions will result in promoters. Detractors, too, can pose significant challenges in your sales efforts. If a customer contact becomes a detractor, they may actively impede your deal within their organization or peer group. As a customer success leader, you must identify promoters and detractors among your customer base and act accordingly.

In the previous chapter, we explored various methods for gathering customer input and feedback. As a customer success leader, it is crucial to continuously monitor this feedback and categorize your customer touchpoints or contacts within their organizations as buyers, consumers, or executors. Furthermore, it is essential to classify them as promoters, detractors, or neutral parties.

Determining whether a customer is a promoter or a detractor can be achieved by assessing their willingness to engage in various activities. These activities include participating in pulse surveys, speaking at events on behalf of your company, or serving as a reference for your prospects. These indicators help gauge the level of satisfaction and loyalty a customer has towards your company. Establishing a program aimed at actively engaging promoters is prudent, ensuring their willingness and availability to support your customer marketing initiatives, including serving as references for your prospects.

However, suppose a customer actively avoids these opportunities and does not respond to repeated invitations. In that case, it may indicate a red flag, suggesting that the customer could be a neutral or even a detractor. In such cases, seeking third-party assistance in obtaining customer feedback becomes advisable, particularly if the customer holds influence or is a critical decision-maker within their organization. For example, if a key decision-maker in a large enterprise company actively avoids communication with you, gathering feedback from alternative sources is advisable. Some companies specialize in conducting discreet interviews, or you can leverage your network to gain insights into the perspective of the executive or key contact. This external feedback can provide valuable insights into any potential issues they may have with your product, personnel, or features.

Understanding key decision-makers and influencers' thoughts and sentiments is essential as it allows you to identify areas for improvement and take necessary actions to strengthen customer relationships. By addressing any underlying problems, you can build better relationships with your customers and improve overall customer satisfaction.

The impact of having a group of passionate promoters who strongly connect with your product and become advocates for it is exponential. They have the power to spread your message throughout the market far more effectively than relying solely on your employees or marketing team. This approach adds authenticity to your product, driven by genuine end-users who believe in it. As a result, your product gains momentum and spreads rapidly like wildfire.

It is also crucial to cultivate promoters because they carry their preferred tools, platforms, or services wherever they go. For instance, if an executive has had a positive experience with your SAAS product or platform within one organization and then transitions to a new organization, they are likely to continue using and advocating for your product based on their previous experience. This loyalty lasts as long as the promoter remains in a position to influence decisions.

Building a strong community is key to effectively engaging with your end users, cultivating a dedicated group of promoters, and establishing regular communication with and among them. The role of a community in the success of B2B SAAS organizations cannot be overstated, as numerous successful companies have thrived with the support of their communities. Salesforce's Trailblazers community stands out as a prime example. Additionally, HubSpot and RocketLane have demonstrated that communities have the power to drive success.

Hence, for any B2B SaaS company to successfully engage a vast group of promoters, it is vital to foster a robust community. This community can serve as a platform for collaboration, knowledge sharing, and building strong relationships. Companies can create a network of loyal advocates who champion their products and services by actively involving and empowering community members. Consistent communication, engagement initiatives, and value-driven interactions are key to nurturing a flourishing community and driving the success of a B2B SaaS organization.

To cultivate thriving communities, utilizing a diverse range of tools is crucial. Adopting a comprehensive strategy encompassing both online and offline channels yields significant benefits. Online platforms, such as dedicated websites or Slack channels, serve as dynamic hubs where users can seamlessly collaborate, share insights, and address challenges they encounter. These digital spaces provide an invaluable arena for diverse perspectives to converge, facilitating the exchange of collective wisdom that transcends individual experiences. Moreover, harnessing the power of online platforms offers a distinct advantage in transcending geographical barriers and rapidly disseminating information. This global reach empowers communities to expand their influence and accelerate progress toward shared objectives.

Moreover, the true essence of a community lies in its ability to address broader issues beyond mere product functionalities. Communities can serve as catalysts for wider industry/functional impact, offering support beyond conventional service offerings. For instance, facilitating job opportunities, functional knowledge improvement, and career advancement initiatives within the community empowers members to thrive collectively. Empowering some of the most active users to moderate and steer the direction of these communities is pivotal for the organic growth and sustainability of the community.

In the evolving landscape of a post-COVID world, the significance of physical connection has become increasingly evident, satisfying a fundamental human need for personal interaction. Offline community engagements, as demonstrated by successful models like Salesforce and Microsoft user groups, provide tangible opportunities for knowledge exchange, networking, and collective celebration. These face-to-face interactions foster deeper connections and propel professional development in ways that digital platforms alone cannot emulate.

Crafting a seamless communication strategy is paramount, whether through drip campaigns, regular updates on product enhancements and roadmap developments, or direct interaction to solicit and respond to feedback. However, a pitfall in community building lies in allowing users to become dormant. Maintaining an active dialogue within the community, initiated by either the organization or its members, is essential to sustain engagement and relevance.

Just as organizations require structured frameworks for coherence and longevity, communities similarly benefit from defined guidelines and moderation. Moderators play a crucial role in ensuring discussions remain focused, professional, and aligned with the community's values and objectives. Whether these moderators are internal employees or community members can be tailored to suit the community's dynamics and goals.

In essence, cultivating online and offline communities unleashes a potent force for collaboration, innovation, and mutual support, enriching the collective journey of all involved. Drawing from my experience, a fundamental step in community building is to allocate dedicated resources specifically for this purpose. Within your organization, it's essential to designate individuals, ideally within the customer success team, solely focused on nurturing the community. This proactive approach ensures the community receives the attention and support it requires to flourish.

When identifying the first few potential community promoters, it is crucial to prioritize quality over quantity. Rather than employing a scattergun approach, seek out individuals who exhibit genuine enthusiasm and commitment towards your organization's goals. These enthusiasts serve as the bedrock of the community, driving its growth and vitality through their authentic engagement.

Key to this process is aligning the community's objectives with the aspirations of its promoters. When the community's mission resonates with individuals' personal or professional goals, they are more inclined to contribute and advocate for its success actively. This alignment cultivates a sense of ownership and investment among promoters, fostering a mutually beneficial relationship.

Another crucial aspect to consider is establishing clear expectations regarding response times within the community. While it may not be necessary for community interactions to adhere strictly to the same standards as formal support organizations, setting and adapting to reasonable expectations is essential. For instance, as a community user, knowing that inquiries will be addressed by the end of the day instills confidence and encourages active participation. During the community's initial stages, clearly defining the anticipated response time is vital. As the community gains momentum and users begin assisting each other, the need for stringent response times may diminish. However, setting expectations early ensures a positive user experience and fosters trust in the community's reliability.

To cultivate a vibrant and dynamic community, it is essential to incentivize active engagement and contribution among its members. Implementing tailored strategies that align with the community's unique dynamics and objectives is key.

Firstly, prioritizing a meritocratic approach is vital. Recognizing and celebrating genuine contributions within the community fosters a sense of accomplishment and encourages continued participation. Take, for instance, the Trailblazer community, where members can attain various rankings, such as triple star ranger. A hierarchical structure becomes aspirational based on merit, effort, and authenticity.

Identifying star contributors who significantly contribute to the community's growth is crucial. Integrating them into your organization's fabric by inviting them to company events, sending them tokens of appreciation, and publicly acknowledging their contributions reinforces their value and commitment.

Additionally, maintaining the exclusivity of the community is essential. You can foster a sense of belonging and cohesion among members by ensuring a clear direction and purpose. A focused community with specific goals will likely thrive and attract like-minded individuals, driving its growth and success.

To ensure that the community seamlessly integrates as an organic extension of your company, exclusivity is key. This entails establishing a dedicated team to oversee community operations. Central to this approach is the implementation of community-related metrics driven by this specialized team. It is essential to define specific metrics to gauge community engagement effectively. Metrics such as community participation, activity frequency, active membership count, and the number of star contributors are invaluable in assessing the community's vitality and growth trajectory. Tracking growth rates on a year-on-year, month-on-month, or quarter-on-quarter basis provides valuable insights into its evolution over time.

Moreover, it is crucial to establish clear targets for community managers aligned with these metrics. This ensures accountability and drives focused efforts towards community growth and enrichment. By integrating the community into the advocacy aspect of your organization, customer success managers and CSMs become integral members of the team.

Another pivotal avenue for promoting advocacy and commemorating customer success is the creation of case studies and press releases. Press releases serve as a means to announce and highlight the partnerships forged with customers, while case studies offer a more comprehensive exploration.

In contrast to press releases, case studies afford greater flexibility in content and format. They are typically structured around specific features, functionalities, or use cases, which can be translated into marketing collateral for prospective customers. As the most authentic method, case studies effectively underscore the value that your features contribute to existing customers, serving as compelling testimonials of your product's efficacy.

One of the approaches that I really found useful during my tenure was the practice of celebrating shared victories with our customers. It is paramount for a B2B SaaS company to acknowledge and celebrate its customers' achievements. For instance, if your company holds a prominent position within a specific industry, it's advantageous to recognize outstanding individuals or organizations within that sector.

A prime example of this approach is seen in the Customer Engagement Excellence Awards organized by MoEngage. These awards spotlighted customers who demonstrated exceptional engagement with their end users, aligning with MoEngage's leadership in the industry. By recognizing and honoring accomplishments within your customer base, you not only strengthen relationships but also inspire other customers and prospects to strive for excellence.

It is imperative to incorporate advocacy metrics into the performance evaluation of Customer Success Managers (CSMs). These metrics serve as leading indicators crucial for driving overarching organizational goals effectively. I have implemented various advocacy-related metrics, such as case studies, press releases, and social media amplification posts, including third-party reviews. However, it is essential to establish specific advocacy-related metrics for CSMs to ensure that advocacy remains a focal point of their efforts. By aligning compensation and performance measurements with advocacy metrics, you reinforce its importance and prioritize its integration into the core responsibilities of CSMs, thereby fostering a culture of advocacy within your organization.

In conclusion, fostering customer advocacy and success is paramount for driving growth and sustainability in any business endeavor. By leveraging existing customer relationships, nurturing promoters, and addressing detractors, organizations can capitalize on advocacy as a fundamental sales driver. Furthermore, building vibrant communities, celebrating shared victories, and integrating advocacy metrics into performance evaluations are essential strategies for cultivating a culture of advocacy within organizations. Through these concerted efforts, businesses can establish trust, drive customer loyalty, and ultimately propel long-term success in the competitive landscape.

10

INTERVIEW: HOW TO BUILD A VIBRANTCOMMUNITY?

Guest: Srikrishnan Ganeshan, Co-founder and CEO, Rocketlane

Introduction

Atma Gunupudi (Atma): Hello Sri, I want to begin this discussion by expressing my sincere gratitude for taking the time to sit down with me and share your expertise on Customer Success, Customer Onboarding, and Community. Despite the demanding and hectic growth stage of your company, you have generously offered your valuable insights, which are not only enlightening but also serve as a source of inspiration for myself and many others in the Customer Success field.

I want to reiterate that your innovative approach to creating a new product and market segment, along with your deep understanding of the industry and product vision, make you an exceptional role model and inspiration to us all.

Srikrishna Ganesan (Sri): It's my pleasure to offer my assistance in any way possible. You have played a significant role in shaping the Customer Success community, and I am always eager to collaborate and share knowledge. We are all on a learning journey, and I have gained valuable insights from individuals like yourself. It's a rewarding experience to engage in this exchange of ideas and continue to grow together.

Atma: Thank you very much. The first question I would like to start with is what is Rocketlane? What is the problem you are solving and why?

Sri: Rocketlane is the leading modern, customer-centric PSA and Client Onboarding platform that helps businesses accelerate their client projects and time-to-value, while improving team utilization and project profitability. The platform replaces legacy PSA and generic project tools with an all-in-one, modern platform. Rocketlane offers a unique, unified workspace that improves communication, collaboration, and project visibility for businesses and their clients. It equips teams with insights and benchmarks across projects, which in turn helps them optimize playbooks and processes. Rocketlane also runs Preflight.cx, the only community focused on implementation and onboarding teams. To learn more about Rocketlane, visit www.rocketlane.com.

Atma: Sri, I'm curious to hear about your unique perspective on Customer Success and what it represents for you as a CEO. While 'customer-first' and 'customer-centric' are common terms we see brandished about, their interpretations can greatly vary among leaders. Could you share your personal philosophy on Customer Success and how it shapes the way you lead your company?

Sri: My understanding of 'Customer Success' extends beyond the formal definition of an individual or organization who has entered into a contractual agreement to use our services. While that marks the official start of their status as a customer, I view our relationship as a journey that begins even before the contract is signed. Prospects are regarded with the same consideration as if they were current customers, and this perspective continues even if they choose to churn. To me, they are not former customers; they remain part of our overarching experience. Therefore, interactions such as canceling an account or transferring data are handled with the same level of customer service and care. It's about providing a consistent and valuable experience at every stage of their journey with us.

Atma: Sri, that's an insightful perspective and it's one that I've observed among many esteemed CEOs, who embody the principle that 'Once a customer, always a customer'. This enduring viewpoint is especially crucial for companies in their nascent stages. Speaking of early stages, the concept of an ICP, or Ideal Customer Persona, is frequently used to guide business strategies. Could you share with us, in your view, who embodies the Ideal Customer Persona for Rocketlane?

Sri: For Rocketlane, defining our Ideal Customer Persona revolves around our vision, acknowledging both the current ICP and the broader ICP we aim to serve in the future. At present, our targeted ICP consists predominantly of services teams situated within product companies—specifically, those teams like implementation or professional services within SaaS or tech companies, which make up about seventy percent of our clientele. The other thirty percent are standalone service companies, ranging from small teams of ten up to larger companies with around 800 members, typically engaged in projects lasting three weeks or longer. Ultimately, our product is designed for any client-facing team that thrives on collaboration and runs customer-facing initiatives.

Atma: Your focus on collaboration as a key highlight of Rocketlane's vision sets the theme for our conversation here on. Firstly, I am impressed with how you have carved out a new market segment, especially since there's a scarcity of predefined roles or titles that align with your ICP. The early days must have been fascinating, as establishing a new product niche and related personas is notably challenging. It involves venturing into areas without established collaborative norms. I'm curious about your initial steps—how did you identify the right individuals and foster this sense of community from the ground up? Creating a community is natural once you have a customer base, but you seemed to have built this even before that milestone. Could you enlighten us on how you pinpointed and connected with the early members of your community?

Sri: In April 2020 when Rocketlane was founded, we began by engaging various stakeholders to understand their perspectives on the problem we aimed to address. This included investors, CEOs, Chief Customer Officers, VPs of Customer Success, leaders of implementation and onboarding teams, and the frontline workers in those roles. We had numerous conversations that revealed diverse priorities and approaches to the early customer journey, highlighting differences in how each company tackled specific challenges.

What emerged was an opportunity for peer learning. For instance, we heard stories about how some companies fine-tuned their kick-off process to set a successful engagement tone, while others developed strategies to keep customers accountable, or streamlined their User Acceptance Testing (UAT) to ensure timely launches. Recognizing that these varied experiences offered valuable insights, the idea of bringing these professionals together to share their knowledge sparked in our minds, though we didn't act on it immediately.

Later that year, a conversation with a founder friend led to a breakthrough. He shared how he reduced his project implementation time from six months to six weeks, detailing tactics that might benefit a broader audience. When I offered his insights to a group of enterprise SaaS founders, the response was overwhelmingly positive, resulting in an impromptu, highly engaging roundtable discussion rather than a typical webinar.

Originally scheduled for less than an hour, the conversation extended to an hour and a half, with the discussion continuing even after the meeting in a Slack group originally intended for a small circle. Witnessing the level of engagement during that first session, we decided to host two such discussions monthly, fostering a community of practice long before our product even launched—nine months prior, in fact.

Atma: What a compelling narrative, Sri. Your determination to listen to customers and address their challenges is truly commendable. With the significance of community now clearly expressed in Rocketlane's foundations, I'm interested to know how you leverage it. Do you view the community primarily as a way to generate prospects or as a means to enhance customer engagement? Or do you have a different approach altogether when it comes to the role of community? Is there a particular aspect—prospects or customers—that you focus more on within the community?

Sri: From day 0 we were very clear that for Rocketlane, community isn't just about prospecting or customer retention but about fostering a culture of knowledge-sharing and learning. The most valuable outcome so far has been the enrichment of our understanding and the expansion of our content. Our community, which we call Preflight, has been a treasure trove of insightful conversations. We've repurposed these dialogues into a series of blog posts known as Preflight Conversations, contributing greatly to our thought leadership.

Our approach to leveraging the community isn't driven by short-term metrics like monthly lead counts—we're playing the long game, focused on long-term gains. While we haven't utilized it as a formal customer community or advisory board yet, it's definitely on our roadmap to create a dedicated space for customers within the wider ecosystem.

Even now, our customers benefit when they seek advice on various topics within their industry, may it be seeking guidance on Rocketlane-specific issues or on broader challenges such as client relations. The community's collective wisdom offers solutions. As a result, we have observed that when our customers achieve success—

whether directly through us or by the support of our community—they link Rocketlane with thought leadership. Ultimately, we become synonymous with enabling a community that champions each other's success.

Atma: It's commendable that you prioritize foundational principles and long-term value over immediate gains. You mentioned how your initial webinar sparked interest and led to organic community growth. Are there any deliberate efforts or tactics you use to attract community members in a more structured way, or is organic growth sufficient for your goals? If you do have strategies for proactive community building, I'm sure our readers would be eager to learn about methods for attracting and recruiting community members.

Sri: In building our community, we've taken a strategic and multifaceted approach, right from the start. During the early days, we conducted surveys and even offered Amazon vouchers as an incentive to engage with our target audience. Once we had established an active base of community members from notable companies, I initiated outreach strategies that were similar to SDR tactics, inviting industry leaders to join and contribute. My focus was on identifying individuals who had successfully navigated the onboarding and implementation arena, encouraging them to share their insights and experiences. Not only did this add immense value to our community, but it also helped to attract further interest.

Aligning sales and marketing efforts around the community has been a key part of our strategy, especially after our product launch. By using event participant lists, we developed email sequences that highlighted the community's benefits, emphasizing the importance of the learning and sharing that takes place within our network. Such efforts have resulted in recognition from industry peers and mentions at various events.

Our sales team, for instance, now regularly talks about the community as a standout feature from the very first call with a prospect, highlighting our thought leadership and establishing our credibility—regardless of the sales outcome. At the same time, the community offers a nurturing environment, which is a boon for our marketing efforts.

We ensure that the value of the community is reinforced at every customer touchpoint, from kickoff calls to training sessions. At events, we also focus on creating a distinct presence for the community, complete with dedicated branding and even the initiation of local chapters for more personalized interactions. Watching how we've nurtured this parallel ecosystem that emphasizes community at every turn, independent of direct sales conversion, has been incredibly fulfilling.

Atma: It's impressive to see how deeply you value the community and make it a priority. Your dedication to creating a positive customer experience while also fostering community engagement is truly remarkable. The integration of sales, marketing, and post-sales teams into community conversations is an excellent example of this.

Regarding the mechanics of running the community, I'm curious about the role of moderators. Do you have dedicated individuals or community leaders who actively engage and manage the community, particularly in situations where negative comments or discussions arise? What are your general guidelines for effective moderation within the community?

Sri: Good question, Atma. I often get asked what we would do if someone were to post something negative in the community, or if there's a mention of a competitor. The truth is, that situation hasn't really arisen. Sure, there are occasional questions or comments, but we handle them discreetly. Our stance is clear: the community is hosted by Rocketlane, but it's not a platform for self-promotion. Direct messages are used for responses that don't pertain to the community at large. Our main focus is on adding value to the community members.

The most crucial aspect we moderate is the community's membership. We want to avoid people joining solely to make sales pitches. This applies to our team as well; we encourage learning and discourage unsolicited sales messages. We also have to be cautious about competitors joining the community. Currently, we don't allow it, to prevent any potential risks or uncomfortable situations. Exceptions are made for certain individuals, like marketers from other companies or fellow founders, who genuinely want to learn about community management. Otherwise, membership is restricted to those who fit the role and can truly gain from what the community has to offer.

Atma: Your emphasis on separating the community from sales and nurturing organic growth is invaluable. It leads me to wonder about the structure of these communities, particularly regarding user personas. Many CEOs and product leaders often ask if there should be a community tailored for specific personas. Do you think there's merit in creating communities specifically for technical users, another for executives, and perhaps another for end users? Or do you believe a mixed-persona community serves a greater purpose?

Sri: In our community, we've established a range of special interest groups that align with the different stages of our members' professional journeys. For instance, there's a group specifically geared towards those in enterprise-level positions, another for individuals interested in high-velocity environments, and a group dedicated to VPs overseeing expansive teams. These groups are invaluable because they allow for discussions that are highly relevant and specific to the members' experiences.

The concept of a 'cracker-reducing' group is intriguing—these groups minimize noise and unnecessary distractions, making the shared knowledge and discussions much more pertinent to the participants. Such focused groups foster an environment where problems and solutions are immediately applicable and relatable. This not only enhances problem-solving within the group but also allows distilled and targeted insights to be shared across a wider audience, greatly beneficial for the entire community.

Atma: Fascinating. As the costs of CS are becoming critical for several CEOs I have observed that the concept of 'velocity motion' and scalable engagement is becoming key. I have also noticed that there's a trend where communities are being leveraged as platforms to engage with a broader customer base at low cost. I'm curious about your perspective on utilizing communities as a means to potentially substitute Customer Success Managers (CSMs) and facilitate engagement at scale. What are your thoughts on the effectiveness of communities in this context, and do you believe they could be a viable alternative to traditional CSM roles?"

Sri: The potential of using communities to enable customer engagement at scale truly comes into play as you hit a certain threshold. Particularly for companies with over 500 customers, and especially those catering to the SMB sector, establishing a customer-focused community can be invaluable. It fosters a support network where customers help each other out. Of course, the concern about negativity and unconstructive conversations is valid. However, that can be managed by setting clear community guidelines upfront. It's crucial to communicate that the community is a space for mutual support and collective problem-solving, not for airing grievances or spreading negativity.

Leveraging tools and practices from open-source communities, which are experienced in moderating large, engaged user bases, can be beneficial. They use specialized tools to monitor discussions, ensuring inquiries are addressed promptly. While we haven't fully implemented this at our end, we're laying the groundwork through collaborative webinars on specific features and capabilities. For example, we recently introduced a major automation feature and conducted a workshop with a group of small customers. This initiative could serve as a springboard for launching a dedicated customer community, creating a more interactive and self-sustaining and engaging environment.

Atma: When it comes to building communities, Sri, what are your top tool recommendations? Apart from Slack and Zoom, are there any other tools you believe can help in effectively engaging large communities?

Sri: We have found Treadoo to be a valuable tool for automating community tasks and keeping track of conversations. However, the choice of platform for building a community depends on the target audience. For instance, if you are reaching out to smaller company users across companies, Slack would be a suitable option as many teams are already using it. On the other hand, if your target customers are enterprises, who primarily use Microsoft Teams, it might not be as effective to create a Slack community. In such cases, it's crucial to consider where your audience already spends their time.

Investing in community-focused tools is also beneficial, especially when building customer communities. These tools help with content publication and ownership, ensuring that valuable information remains accessible over time. While we have managed to save content through Treadoo and regularly publish learnings in our Slack community, it is advisable to invest in a dedicated platform for this purpose. Each platform has its own set of advantages and disadvantages in terms of engaging users and bringing them back. Pick a platform that can be used in the long term as once you select a platform, it can be challenging to transition to a new one due to the concern of whether everyone will migrate along.

Atma: Sri, given the significant increase in online collaboration, communities, and tools during the COVID-19 pandemic, I'm curious about your thoughts on offline communities in the new "new" normal where people are gradually returning to in-person meetings.

Do you believe offline communities are still essential in this digital age? Additionally, could you share your insights on the percentage of users who prefer offline community meetups, considering the potential resource-intensive nature of organizing such events?

Sri: Offline communities still hold value in this digital age, especially for individuals seeking new opportunities in the job market. Bringing people together in person can be beneficial from a networking perspective. Many companies are often willing to provide their space for hosting community meetups, making it essential to reach out to the right individuals and establish partnerships or sponsorships to facilitate such events.

Offline communities offer the opportunity to connect individuals who can derive value from each other. While it may not be feasible for your team to travel to every location, a viable approach is to empower community members in different cities to organize and host events themselves. We have volunteers in 17 different cities who willingly contribute to organizing these events.

We have found a format that proves highly effective, wherein we invite three founders who are experiencing specific challenges. Participants are divided into groups and engage in brainstorming sessions to provide real-world solutions to these founders' problems. It essentially becomes a workshop session, culminating in idea presentations that offer valuable learning experiences for everyone involved. Additionally, we have also conducted panel discussions and various other formats that have proven valuable for the community. Ultimately, anything that brings benefit to the individuals in our community is something we strive to continue doing.

Atma: Thank you once again for the insightful conversation on customer obsession and the importance of community. Before we conclude, could you please share any advice or key insights you have for young customer success leaders or startup founders who are in the process of setting up their customer success functions?

Sri: When it comes to setting up customer success functions, my advice for young CS leaders or startup founders would be to first establish a clear vision. Have meaningful conversations and build a shared understanding of what you aim to achieve with your team even before hiring them. It is crucial to determine the market segment you are targeting, whether it's SMBs, the mid-market, or any other specific niche. This will help you understand the type of team you need to build and align your strategies accordingly. Consider factors such as monthly renewals versus annual renewals, and anticipate where your product will be in the next two years.

Hiring the right people based on this vision is vital. Make sure to set expectations with your team members, letting them know that their roles may evolve as the company grows. For example, a CS role that starts as one may expand into multiple roles, such as support, customer success implementation, etc. This gives individuals a clear understanding of their current position and potential future growth within the organization.

Geographically, I would specifically recommend Indian startup founders to consider overinvesting in customer success early on. The affordable cost structure in India provides an opportunity to build a strong CS team, and it can also serve as an area of differentiation for your startup. By focusing on providing exceptional customer success experiences, you can set yourself apart from competitors and build a strong foundation for future growth.

Atma: Thank you sincerely, Sri, for dedicating your time and sharing your valuable insights. I greatly appreciate your effort and contribution to our conversation.

11

PART III: THE TEAM

In this section of the book, we will examine the critical aspects of building high-performance teams within B2B SaaS customer success organizations. We will outline some key components integral to such teams and provide insights drawn from extensive industry experience.

Customer Success Management (CSM): CSMs lead the charge in fostering lasting client relationships and ensuring value realization. They focus on understanding client needs and providing ongoing guidance to the customer so that they can maximize platform value.

Account Management: These teams drive product and revenue growth within client organizations by identifying upselling and cross-selling opportunities. By aligning with clients' evolving needs and objectives, they strengthen partnerships. Digital Success: Dedicated to the long tail customers, these teams prioritize scalability and cost-effectiveness through digital channels and automation tools, ensuring a positive experience at scale. Success Programs: These teams orchestrate one-to-many engagement initiatives, such as training programs and webinars, to empower clients and enhance satisfaction through knowledge dissemination.

Professional Services and Managed Services: Professional Services teams, including Implementation and Onboarding specialists, ensure smooth platform integration and user adoption. They work closely with clients to customize the platform to their specific needs and provide hands-on support throughout the implementation process. Managed Services teams offer additional execution support, streamlining customer operations and ensuring ongoing success.

These components, along with Technical Account Management, Business Consulting, Support Organizations, Revenue Management, and Success Marketing teams, form a comprehensive framework for building high-performance customer success teams. Effective team segmentation strategies, including regional, revenue-based, and industry-focused approaches, enable organizations to tailor their customer success efforts and drive sustainable growth in the competitive B2B SaaS landscape.

12

SAAS SUCCESS: CRAFTING HIGH-PERFORMANCE TEAMS

In this chapter, I will endeavor to detail the intricacies of team structure and composition within B2B SaaS companies' customer success organizations. Drawing from my extensive experience managing, building, and leading such teams, I will guide you through the five major components typically found in these setups.

At the core of any customer success organization lies the team responsible for nurturing ongoing customer relationships, often referred to as the Customer Success Management team. Central to this team is the role of the customer success manager. The titles may vary across organizations, ranging from customer outcome managers, customer engagement managers, and customer value managers to customer relationship managers, based on the phase of the company and the way they manage their customers' recurring revenue. Regardless of nomenclature, their primary focus remains consistent: fostering and maintaining strong customer connections, understanding their objectives and requirements, and facilitating optimal returns on investment for customers from your platform or product. Customer success managers are pivotal in ensuring customers adopt and utilize your solutions effectively and realize maximum value.

Another element within the customer success function is Account Management. Acting as both hunters and farmers, account managers are tasked with cultivating enduring relationships, managing customer satisfaction, and driving product expansion within client organizations, often guided by set quotas. This team comprises individuals with sales profiles who primarily manage upsell and cross-sell motions for your organization.

Another component of the customer success team gaining prominence in many organizations in recent times is the Digital Success team. Comprising specialized resources with centralized expertise in specific facets of our product or platform, they provide targeted assistance and guidance to customers encountering challenges or seeking best practices. These resources are deployed predominantly for lower-dollar value customers and operate remotely, thereby optimizing resource allocation and cost-effectiveness. Furthermore, the rise of digital success teams underscores a shift towards scalable and cost-effective resource deployment.

Another essential group within customer success teams contributing to a scalable customer success delivery approach is the Success Programs team. This team focuses on one-to-many customer engagement initiatives. These teams facilitate knowledge dissemination through webinars, workshops, and best practice sessions, efficiently addressing diverse customer needs. Organizations enhance customer satisfaction and expand their reach by combining expertise in specific product features with broader programmatic initiatives.

Now, let us explore the second function of the customer success organization, which is the professional services team. These teams comprise various roles and exhibit diverse compositions. The pivotal role among them is that of Implementation teams. Essentially, these teams guide the customer from day one to the day they go live with your application or beyond. They ensure your customer can effectively utilize your platform, product, or service to achieve their desired outcomes. Typically led by solution consulting managers, these teams aim to replicate successful solutions implemented with similar customers, often leveraging predefined playbooks. The implementation team serves as the initial interface between the customer and your company, guiding them to leverage the platform and reap its benefits fully.

Another integral part of professional services is the Onboarding team. These individuals are responsible for setting up the customer's organizational structures, security metrics, roles, responsibilities, and data access. They conduct product walkthroughs and provide training to ensure customers are equipped to utilize the platform effectively. While the implementation team focuses on the technical aspects of product or platform integration, the onboarding team specializes in change management, ensuring smooth transitions and proper setup from both learning and product usage perspectives.

In addition to these functions, many organizations, especially B2B SaaS companies, employ Managed Services teams to enhance the customer experience further. These teams not only gain access to the platform but also undertake execution tasks, either from the customer or the service provider. For instance, a campaign execution team could work on customers' engagement platforms and deliver campaigns, serving as an excellent example of managed services. They might deploy automated lead rotation or execute certain lead management tasks on platforms like Salesforce. These teams go beyond platform implementation, handling tasks typically carried out by customers on the platform. This eliminates the need for customers to hire, maintain, and manage resources with in-depth technical knowledge and functional knowledge about the industry and platform. If customers can access these managed services at a relatively lower cost compared to hiring, training, and continuously updating resources, then utilizing these services becomes a convenient option for them.

Another aspect of professional services involves Customization. Traditionally, organizations tend to avoid heavily customizing their products in the realm of B2B SaaS due to the challenges they pose for support, maintenance, and scalability. It is often a complex proposition for B2B SaaS companies to scale while heavily customizing products for individual users or customers. To address this challenge, I have observed B2B SaaS companies deploying development teams to customer sites for customization and subsequent maintenance efforts. Their role is to tailor specific parts of the broader product to meet each customer's unique needs, ensuring alignment with their requirements. Subsequently, these engineers often remain with the customer to maintain the customized build and fine-tune the customizations as needed. Typically, these customization teams operate as hybrid organizations, comprising team members from the SaaS provider and the customer. This collaborative approach ensures that both parties contribute resources and expertise to achieve the desired customization outcomes.

Another vital component of the professional services team is the Technical Account Management (TAM) team. These are dedicated resources assigned to accounts post-go-live. While the onboarding and implementation teams ensure a successful platform or product launch, there may still be ongoing requirements from the customer's end, such as minor fixes to configurations or further implementation of new use cases. For such needs, larger customers often retain a technical account manager with technical expertise and customer care skills. These resources assist customers in various ways, including debugging code on both the customer and service provider sides, providing technical and implementation best practices, or preparing customers for their upcoming peak season. This hands-on support ensures that customers receive continued assistance and guidance after the initial implementation phase.

Lastly, we have the Business Consulting team, which is an integral part of the professional services team. These team members are typically industry experts specializing in business consulting. They pivot away from technical minutiae or product features, instead offering the customer comprehensive business solutions and guidance. Their focus extends to addressing broader business challenges using your platform or tool. These teams typically provide blueprints that guide implementation teams in conducting in-depth technical analyses and executing implementations. The business consulting team guides use cases, operating at a level above the specific tech product. Their expertise lies in understanding the customer's business objectives and aligning them with the capabilities of the platform or tool.

The third pillar of the customer success organization is the Support Organization. Essentially, the support organization collaborates with the customer throughout their relationship with your company, ensuring the resolution of tactical product/technical issues. Composed of highly technical individuals, this team typically requires an in-depth understanding of your product and technology stack and the ability to grasp customer implementation quickly, use cases, and specific tasks. Their expertise lies in possessing a comprehensive knowledge of your product and platform, particularly regarding typical issues faced by customers. Support organizations vary in their structure and approach.

Depending on the complexity of the product, the maturity of the company, and the scale of the support organization, there could be several teams within the support organization. Here, we will cover a few of them. The first component is the Technical Support team, where problem-solving experts, known for their debugging skills, tackle customer issues. They identify and debug problems, whether they arise from the customer's code or your company's side, ensuring timely resolution. This team often includes Technical Support Engineers with backgrounds in engineering and technology.

Next, there are functional support teams. Depending on your organization's maturity, you may leverage Customer Success Managers (CSMs) for these activities or opt for in-house operational support functions to save resources. Functional support teams guide customers through documentation and assist with non-technical inquiries, such as feature usage, platform needs, etc.

The third team is the Escalation Management and Incident Management Team, both integral parts of technical support. While they share the goal of resolving complex issues, their roles differ. The escalation management team intervenes in prolonged issues, redirecting technical resources or prioritizing specific actions to ensure key customer resolution. Conversely, the incident management team swiftly deploys resources during major platform incidents, ensuring undivided attention on issue resolution and providing regular customer updates.

Finally, a robust support team needs a strong operational team. This team analyzes data, identifies trends and gaps, and manages bandwidth, utilization, and projects. These operations teams can be centralized or integrated into technical support and customer success teams. Based on my experience, I strongly recommend investing in operations and strategy teams that leverage data insights to solve future challenges proactively.

Now, let us explore another crucial aspect of a successful organization: the Revenue Management team. In any B2B company, as we've discussed, the customer success organization is the guardian of the recurring revenue. Therefore, this function may be integrated within the customer success team or operate independently. Regardless, a team must diligently oversee customer billing, review invoices, identify risks, and proactively manage renewal workflows with actions scheduled three months, two months, and one month before renewal. Additionally, this team actively engages with customers on payment matters, negotiating any discount requests they may have. The size of this team can vary, ranging from a small one or two-member team to a larger one, depending on your customer base and revenue volume.

Finally, let us emphasize the importance of the Success Marketing team. This team plays a pivotal role in amplifying your success stories and promoting your brand's achievements. They ensure that the wider world recognizes the outcomes driven by your success management team. The Success Marketing team can be further divided into subgroups. One subgroup may focus strictly on developing community strategy, recognizing the significance of customer feedback and community engagement. Building and maintaining a vibrant community requires dedicated effort and resources. Another vital aspect of customer marketing is advocacy. This team can work with your Customer Success Managers (CSMs) to generate case studies, press releases, and best practice guidance based on individual customer requirements and transform this material into easily digestible content for external publication, enabling other customers to benefit from these insights. Moreover, your company's sales team can leverage this resource to attract more prospects.

Another crucial aspect of successful marketing is the Success Events team, often underrated yet immensely impactful. Many companies overlook the importance of investing in a dedicated success events team. However, I strongly advocate for the development of a solid customer success event calendar. Celebrating customer milestones with a broader audience is vital. It is also essential for company leadership to engage directly with customers, hosting customer-centric events like executive dinners. Enhancing customer engagement deserves more attention, as it allows companies to celebrate their customers' victories. Therefore, building a dedicated events team is critical.

Now, let us discuss how you can effectively segment your teams. Organizations employ various scales and types of team structures. If your organization primarily operates from a solid home base but serves customers in other countries or regions, consider segmenting your customer success teams based on areas. Typically, this involves prioritizing regions with the highest concentration of customers, such as the Asia Pacific, followed by Europe, the Middle East, and then the Americas, depending on your expansion plans.

As your customer base grows, especially reaching 1000 customers, consider implementing revenue segmentation. This approach entails tailoring strategies for different customer segments, such as SMBs, mid-market customers, and top-paying customers. Recognize that a one-size-fits-all approach is no longer effective. Instead, segment based on the revenue each customer generates or the value they bring to your product, service, or platform. This may lead to segmentation based on top accounts, mid-market accounts, and SMBs.

As your organization expands further and develops specialized solutions for specific industries, consider implementing industry segmentation. This involves creating segments tailored to industries such as banking and financial services, manufacturing, retail, hospitality, and health sciences, among others. However, industry segmentation is only beneficial if your services and products effectively cater to these specific industries and you have significantly different products for different industries.

In conclusion, this chapter has provided an in-depth exploration of the intricacies surrounding team structure and composition within B2B SaaS companies' customer success organizations. Drawing from extensive experience in managing, building, and leading such teams, we have navigated through the five major components typically found in these setups.

From the pivotal roles of Customer Success Managers and Account Managers to the emerging importance of Digital Success and Success Programs teams, we have dissected each function's significance in driving customer satisfaction and retention. Furthermore, we have elucidated the critical roles Professional Services teams play, encompassing Implementation, Onboarding,

Managed Services, Customization, Technical Account Management, and Business Consulting, each contributing to a comprehensive customer success delivery approach.

Additionally, we have underscored the pivotal role of the Support Organization in swiftly resolving technical issues and highlighted the importance of a robust operational team to ensure efficient resource management. Furthermore, we have shed light on the essential function of Revenue Management, emphasizing the diligent oversight required for billing, renewal management, and payment negotiations.

Lastly, we have emphasized the indispensable role of the Success Marketing team in amplifying success stories and promoting brand achievements, along with the significance of hosting success events to enhance customer engagement. Moreover, we provided insights into effective team segmentation strategies, urging organizations to tailor their approaches based on regional, revenue, and industry considerations.

By understanding and implementing these nuanced team structures and segmentation strategies, B2B SaaS companies can cultivate strong customer relationships, drive sustainable growth, and ultimately thrive in an increasingly competitive market landscape.

13

LEADERSHIP EXCELLENCE FOR CUSTOMER SUCCESS

In this chapter, my aim is to provide a comprehensive analysis of the process and steps necessary to effectively identify strong leaders for various functions within your customer success organization. With over two decades of experience in this field, I will primarily focus on the hiring aspect, offering insights on engaging leaders in the critical areas of Customer Success, Technical Support, and Professional Services. Drawing from my personal experience of hiring more than forty leaders across different functions and collaborating with numerous exceptional leaders in each area, I have developed a systematic approach to this process. Within this chapter, we will explore the key characteristics and foundational areas that should be considered when hiring leaders for each of these crucial roles.

The field of Customer Success is relatively new and can vary greatly from one organization to another, making it difficult to evaluate and compare candidates based solely on their resumes. To complicate matters, there is an abundance of references claiming experience in customer success, which can further blur the lines of qualification. Through my extensive experience in interviewing, I have encountered individuals who have held diverse roles, ranging from customer support to account management and coordination, all of which have been loosely labeled as customer success. In certain instances, even program managers have misrepresented themselves as customer success managers, which is inaccurate. Based on my personal experience, I have pinpointed five crucial areas to prioritize when hiring a customer success leader. By taking these areas into consideration, you can make an informed decision and select a leader who possesses the essential expertise and skills to drive optimal results for both your organization and your customers.

An essential attribute of a successful Customer Success leader is a genuine obsession with driving customer success. It is imperative that leaders in this role consistently prioritize and demonstrate a customer-centric approach in all aspects of their work, including important meetings, decision-making, and prioritization. This unwavering focus on the customer is crucial for delivering exceptional customer experiences and driving long-term success for both the customers and the organization. To identify leaders who possess a true dedication to customer success, a valuable technique is to ask candidates to share their experiences and insights regarding customer innovations and losses they have encountered. A customer-obsessed leader will effortlessly align themselves with their customers, taking immense pride in their customers' achievements and feeling a deep regret for any setbacks experienced. They do not view customers as separate entities but rather take personal ownership of their success or failure, understanding that they represent the customers' interests. This level of dedication and alignment with customers is a vital characteristic to seek in a Customer Success leader.

When hiring a Customer Success leader, assessing their ability to effectively manage a portfolio of accounts is crucial. Successful Customer Success leaders possess the skill to allocate their time and resources efficiently among their portfolio of customers. They excel at providing the appropriate level of attention to each customer at the right moment.

Effective portfolio management goes beyond simply dividing attention equally among customers or solely focusing on their financial value or reputation. Instead, it involves strategically segmenting customers into logical groups. This segmentation enables Customer Success leaders to effectively manage and prioritize their interactions across a potentially extensive customer base, which may include hundreds of customers. By employing this strategic approach, Customer Success leaders can ensure that the needs and expectations of all customers are met, leading to overall customer satisfaction and revenue expansion.

In the realm of customer success, a portfolio denotes a collective of customers managed by a designated team. This portfolio is typically structured around various parameters, including geographical location, industry, customer scale, or revenue. For instance, a portfolio manager might oversee customers in specific regions like India or South America or within particular segments such as SMB customers. The pivotal factor lies in the manager's adept allocation of time and attention across the customers within their portfolio.

When assessing potential candidates, it is imperative to grasp their methodology for prioritizing customers within their portfolio. This selection process shouldn't hinge solely on one factor. Still, it should encompass a blend of elements such as revenue, market suitability, strategic significance, industry sway, the provided solution, and the underlying problem your company endeavors to address. Ensuring that the leader's prioritization aligns harmoniously with your company's values and priorities is paramount. Furthermore, it is paramount to ascertain that prospective candidates possess a proven track record in effectively managing portfolios of comparable size or even larger ones akin to what they would oversee within your organization. This assessment factors in projected growth and ensures the candidate's adeptness in navigating the potential complexities that may emerge as your company scales its operations.

The third criterion to consider is proficiency in customer success operations. Customer Success is a relatively new field, and finding leaders with hands-on B2B SaaS Customer Success experience can be difficult. To distinguish between leaders with experience and those with theoretical knowledge, it's essential to assess their grasp of success and recurring revenue operations, as well as key indicators and strategies. Examine the specific leading and lagging indicators the candidate may have utilized to gauge their team's performance effectively. Proactively addressing issues like churn prevention or revenue growth is critical. To assess account risk, a seasoned Customer Success leader relies on various metrics, ranging from usage engagement, stakeholder movement, and key player engagement to indicators like delayed invoice payments or renewals. Validating a candidate's credibility involves probing into the strategies, levers, or mechanisms they employ to impact these crucial metrics positively. Additionally, inquire about their techniques tailored to your organization's specific contexts, economic climates, or regional nuances.

The fourth essential skill to look for in a candidate is technical depth. In today's landscape, a B2B SaaS company leader or a high-tech organization must understand technology. Effective CS leadership typically requires solid technical acumen. Hiring leaders who are well-acquainted with your company's technology stack and ecosystem is advantageous. A critical aspect of a CS leader's success lies in efficiently allocating time and resources between customers and addressing their issues. Hiring a leader who cannot discern the complexity and urgency of customer needs risks undermining the effectiveness of your customer success organization.

Furthermore, B2B SaaS CS executives will spend significant time with customers' technical points of contact, including CTOs, field experts, and product leaders who influence purchasing decisions. If a CS leader cannot engage in meaningful conversations and add value to technical discussions, it diminishes their credibility. Evaluating candidates' technical depth involves examining their experiences with technical challenges, decisions, obstacles, and successes, providing specific and detailed examples.

Another vital skill essential for CS leaders in today's market is sales acumen. Customer Success is becoming a significant revenue driver for B2B and SaaS companies. Maximizing revenue growth from existing customer bases is imperative, requiring CS leaders to understand sales processes profoundly. Recruiting CS leaders with a strong grasp of Product-Market Fit and critical use cases is prudent. Prior startup experience can provide valuable insights, as startup executives often bring sales or pre-sales expertise. Leaders experienced in carrying quotas can instill crucial sales discipline within the organization, thereby fostering sustained revenue growth.

Lastly, people leadership is an essential skill for every customer success leader. While there's abundant literature on leadership traits, in my experience, leaders who advanced through the CS ranks and demonstrate empathy tend to hit the ground running sooner. It is crucial to ensure a leader's core values align with your company and team's ethos. One effective method I've used in evaluating leaders' people leadership skills is to ask about three instances where they promoted individuals, exploring their reasons for selection and the traits they prioritized. This offers valuable insight into their leadership style and values.

Opting for candidates with entrepreneurial experience proves highly beneficial for startups due to their sense of ownership, customer-centric approach, and adeptness in navigating ambiguity. This encapsulates the essentials for hiring Customer Success leadership.

When hiring the right support leader, there are five key skills to prioritize. Drawing from my experience directly managing and working within technical support in B2B SaaS organizations and collaborating with top-tier support leaders in the industry, I have identified essential qualities to seek in a support leader.

First and foremost, their people leadership skills are paramount given that technical support teams often deal with customer issues on the frontline, engaging in transactional interactions. A successful support leader must exhibit empathy and prioritize the well-being of their team members. Effective support leaders I have encountered possess a unique language and approach, consistently putting their team's needs first, even subconsciously, in every situation. They excel at navigating high-stress environments. In addition, great support leaders focus on solutions over problems, addressing process gaps rather than personnel issues. Before hiring a support leader, it is crucial to consider whether your team would be enthusiastic about working with them.

The second crucial skill you should seek in a support leader is their operational rigor. Technical support relies heavily on operational efficiency. The incoming support leader must possess a comprehensive understanding and hands-on experience in optimizing your team into a well-oiled, smoothly operating, and scalable unit. Regardless of the organization's maturity or data accuracy, every effective support leader should prioritize essential leading and lagging indicators and devise strategies to enhance them. They should clearly understand how, where, and when to acquire the right data and insights critical for improving the function. Support leaders' common metrics include customer satisfaction, first response time, SLA adherence, resolution time, agent throughput, and first call resolution.

What distinguishes a good leader is their understanding of critical steps to enhance team performance. To assess this, present them with an underperforming metric in your company and ask for two or three strategies they would propose to improve that specific score. This provides insight into their problem-solving approach and experience. Furthermore, candidates' proficiency with support operations tools is crucial. Given the array of available tools like Zendesk, Freshdesk, and Zoho, hiring a leader who is well-versed in one or more of these platforms is important.

The third essential skill, arguably the most crucial, is technical understanding and problem-solving ability. A proficient level of technical knowledge is paramount for the success of a tech support leader. It can be incredibly frustrating for support engineers and managers to work with someone who does not understand the daily complexities they encounter. Additionally, with a solid grasp of technical issues, it becomes easier for the leader to effectively evaluate, coach, and guide team members. While a support leader can be an expert in some technology, they should possess a foundational understanding across various domains.

Numerous accomplished support leaders have dedicated significant time to advancing within their support teams. Technical support demands individuals with outstanding problem-solving skills, empathy, and a sense of urgency to thrive in their roles, qualities that are often cultivated through firsthand experience and progression within a support organization.

Escalation management is yet another crucial skill to seek in a support leader. On average, a support leader must allocate 15 to 20% of their time and bandwidth to handling escalations. However, this percentage tends to be higher in startups or companies experimenting with new product-market fit. It is integral for the support leader to be willing to invest the effort and roll up their sleeves when dealing with escalations. Escalation management is essential for two main reasons: firstly, to ensure the prompt resolution of the issue at hand, thereby controlling any potential damage and allowing the customer's business to return to normal as swiftly as possible. Secondly, it is vital to identify process gaps that led to the escalation and take steps to address them.

The ability to stay calm and guide a large team during an escalation or crisis is a skill and a personality trait. In tech support, three common personality types emerge when faced with escalations: the "fight" mode leaders, who immediately dive into escalations and actively work to resolve them; the "flight" mode leaders, who prefer to push or delegate escalations to the appropriate team; and the "freeze" mode leaders, who delay addressing escalations altogether. Assessing a candidate's personality based on their approach to escalations is crucial. Ideally, you want someone who demonstrates a "fight" mentality, tackling escalations head-on or exhibiting a "flight" response by efficiently delegating tasks. However, avoiding hiring individuals who show a "freeze" response is crucial. These are individuals who may know the necessary actions but fail to take them due to discomfort or inexperience with high-pressure situations.

The final crucial aspect to consider in a support leader is their ability to drive process improvements. As previously mentioned, technical support operations are highly procedural, and even top-tier support teams have room for enhancement. There are various avenues through which support teams can enhance their efficiency, including automation, utilization of out-of-the-box tools, case-deflection strategies, and training initiatives. Assessing the potential value a new leader can bring to process improvement is essential. You can gauge their ability to enhance processes based on the structure of their thought process and the attention to detail they demonstrate during your discussions.

In addition to the aforementioned qualities, candidates' attitudes, work ethic, cultural fit, and ability to lead by example are equally significant. While relying on references is essential for all positions you are hiring for in support, seeking solid references, including 360-degree review is particularly crucial. A subpar support leader can significantly impact the team's performance and tarnish the organization's culture, potentially taking years to rectify. Therefore, thoroughly evaluating and considering these factors is paramount to selecting the right support leader.

Moving forward to the third segment, as discussed in earlier chapters, Professional Services encompasses a range of components, including onboarding, implementation, managed services, customization, technical account management, and business consulting. Hiring a proficient professional services leader is as challenging as hiring any executive. Below are a few essential characteristics to seek in such a leader:

First and foremost, a professional services leader must possess the necessary technical depth to grasp technology, understand architecture, and stay updated on the latest advancements in the field. Technical proficiency is indispensable for this role. Reflect on whether you feel confident entrusting this individual to lead your engineering teams. If not, exercise caution when considering them for a leadership position in professional services. I emphasize on the importance of highly technical professional services leaders, as an inexperienced leader in this area can undermine the value customers derive from your platform and put the entire organization's success at risk.

The second critical skill for a professional services leader is their ability to provide solutions for complex customer issues. When faced with challenges, corner cases, or customer limitations, a professional services leader should adeptly address them by leveraging the features and functionalities of your product and platform. Additionally, they should demonstrate creativity by proposing innovative solutions to resolve customers' unique situations. Leaders who solely rely on existing products and features without exploring new approaches to tailor solutions may not effectively fulfill their roles in professional services. It is important to note that a leader who rigidly adheres to your features, regardless of the customer's needs or outcomes, may not be suitable for professional services roles. The hallmark of a successful professional services leader is their ability to adapt and innovate to meet the diverse needs of customers.

The third critical skill to seek in a PS Leader is architectural expertise. Professional services leaders must be able to comprehend customer architecture, tech stack, and dependencies quickly. If a PS leader lacks this understanding upon entering a customer organization, they risk being blindsided by critical dependencies and roadblocks. This oversight can prolong implementations by several months, ultimately leading to customer dissatisfaction and damaging your reputation. A PS Leader must possess profound architectural experience within your industry. Navigating challenges effectively becomes considerably more difficult without a thorough understanding of the typical tech stack.

The fourth essential skill is an understanding of the economics involved in professional services, also known as P&L leadership. An experienced services leader should be adept at comprehending their business's profit and loss statement. They must optimize the time and resources of their team to maximize company revenue. This entails understanding various methods and structures for contract writing, execution arrangements, pricing determination, and billing management. The leader we hire should thoroughly understand how work orders, service agreements, and other related materials are written, executed, and managed to ensure that customers receive the correct value while maximizing company revenue.

Additional qualities to look for in professional services leaders include strong people management and practice-building skills. Experienced leaders should dedicate at least 20-30% of their time to building and developing the practice. This entails providing technical challenges to their teams, keeping them abreast of the latest technology trends in the market and among customers, and continuously refining their skills. Practice development plays a crucial role in enhancing the people management abilities of professional services leaders.

In conclusion, this chapter has provided an in-depth analysis of the process and steps necessary to identify strong leaders across various functions within your customer success organization. Drawing from over two decades of experience in this field, I have offered insights into engaging leaders in critical areas such as Customer Success, Technical Support, and Professional Services.

Throughout this chapter, we explored key characteristics and foundational areas crucial for hiring leaders in each of these roles. From customer obsession and portfolio management in Customer Success to technical understanding and escalation management in Technical Support, and from architectural expertise to P&L leadership in Professional Services, we delved into the essential skills and qualities necessary for success in each domain.

By focusing on the customer-centric approach, strategic portfolio management, technical acumen, sales proficiency, people leadership, and process improvement, organizations can effectively identify and onboard leaders who drive optimal results and foster long-term success for both the company and its customers.

As the customer success landscape continues to evolve, prioritizing these skills and qualities will be instrumental in navigating challenges, driving growth, and ensuring customer satisfaction. With a thorough understanding of these key areas, organizations can confidently build and nurture high-performing teams led by capable and impactful leaders.

By leveraging the insights shared in this chapter, organizations can position themselves for success in today's competitive and dynamic market landscape, delivering value to customers and driving sustainable growth in the process.

14

THE POWER OF THE CUSTOMER FLYWHEEL

In this chapter, I aim to explore the transformative concept of the customer flywheel, discussing its various phases, the crucial role played by your customer success team in revenue generation, and the collaboration between account management and customer success teams in achieving tangible outcomes.

Let's begin by dissecting the essence of the customer flywheel. At its core, the customer flywheel embodies creating a dynamic and self-reinforcing cycle, orchestrating customer engagement, retention, and growth. Cultivating a cohort of delighted customers fosters organic growth and enhances the overall market reputation. These satisfied customers evolve into fervent advocates, propelling your product or service through word-of-mouth referrals and expanding your customer base. This virtuous cycle perpetuates, fostering loyalty, increasing usage, and driving substantial revenue gains.

The symbiotic relationship between customer satisfaction and business growth is palpable at each stage of the customer flywheel lifecycle. Every touchpoint with the customer, across various teams within your organization, contributes to nurturing this cycle. By prioritizing customer satisfaction and fostering robust engagement, each interaction becomes a catalyst for perpetuating customer success and business expansion.

Reflecting on my professional journey, I have discerned three dimensions within this perpetual motion: organic revenue addition through expanded usage, inorganic revenue addition via additional revenue streams from the same customer base, and the pivotal amplification of value generated through customer marketing. As we navigate these dimensions, we will uncover actionable strategies and best practices to optimize each stage of the customer flywheel, ensuring sustained growth and fostering enduring customer loyalty.

First and foremost, let us explore the concept of organic revenue, which originates directly from satisfied customers. This revenue stream is sustained over the long term by existing customers who find value in your product, feature, or platform. Organic revenue signifies a consistent flow of income from customers who choose to continue their patronage, sometimes even paying more for the same offerings. This phenomenon, often termed organic growth, indicates a symbiotic relationship between your product and customer base.

Organic growth manifests in various ways, primarily through product expansion linked to customer growth. This expansion could involve the acquisition of additional licenses or adopting consumption-based pricing models, where increased usage translates directly into increased revenue. Additionally, incorporating renewable and adjustable models (RAMs) into your product usage plans ensures a steady revenue increase aligned with your customers' long-term success.

Moreover, organic growth encompasses scenarios where existing customers experience continual growth, leading to a corresponding increase in revenue. However, it is essential to distinguish between genuine organic growth and cost escalations associated with the business environment. While some B2B enterprises opt for renewal escalations to offset rising operational costs, this reflects the cost of doing business rather than organic growth per se. While renewal escalations may contribute to revenue growth, they are not strictly classified as organic. Nonetheless, they underscore the dynamic nature of maintaining sustainable business operations in an evolving market landscape. It is not uncommon for large enterprises to incorporate renewal escalations, typically ranging from five to ten percent every couple of years, to sustain cost escalations and ensure continued service excellence.

The second aspect of revenue growth through customer success is considered inorganic. This can be classified into two types of additional revenue stemming from existing customers. The first type involves expanding into different business units, subsidiaries, or affiliated organizations of the customer. For example, if a product/service is initially sold to one subsidiary within a conglomerate and then extended to other subsidiaries or diverse geographical regions within the same global organization, this expansion generates additional revenue. The second type of inorganic expansion involves selling different products to the same customer. These products may be related or tangential, but the key is the ability to upsell additional products and features to the existing customer base. For instance, if a customer already uses Salesforce's Sales Cloud and the Salesforce team successfully sells additional products like Service Cloud or Marketing Cloud to the same customer.

There are several strategies for implementing inorganic sales within an organization. While outbound and inbound teams, along with account executives, usually concentrate on acquiring new customers, the customer success team plays a crucial role in generating additional revenue from existing customers. Unlike traditional sales methods, customer success managers (CSMs) act as trusted advisors, providing insights and recommendations on new products or features that could benefit the customer. This personalized approach often leads to higher customer engagement and acceptance than standard sales outreach efforts, primarily focused on revenue.

Consider the scenario of inbound calls. Who do you believe the customer would prefer to contact first if they are interested in a new product or service: a sales executive from a competitor or your CSM? It is evident that the CSM stands a better chance of getting an audience with the key customer contact than anyone else. Consider this carefully: in both inbound and outbound interactions, the CSM is more likely to engage with the customer, whether to share an idea or to understand the customer's interests, compared to an account executive reaching out to a prospective customer. This dynamic is feasible only in organizations where the CSM functions as a trusted advisor. However, it is crucial to note that just because the customer is receptive and the CSM has their attention, it doesn't imply that every product or service should be pushed for sale. This is why when leveraging customer success teams for sales purposes, the CSM must first ascertain the customer's needs, budget, and timeline before presenting any proposals. It is essential for the CSM to discern whether the customer truly requires the product or feature being offered.

It is paramount for CSMs to grasp the customer's budgetary constraints and understand the approximate timeline for product or feature adoption. By aligning with these two key factors, it becomes easier to tailor proposals effectively. Continuously pitching ideas without considering these aspects can prove counterproductive, potentially eroding trust and increasing the risk of churn or diminished confidence.

The third avenue for the customer success team to boost additional revenue involves cultivating more customer references, which is a powerful multiplier. A single satisfied customer has the potential to influence dozens, even hundreds, of others within their network, encouraging them to consider your product, platform, or service. Therefore, it is imperative for success teams to drive adoption actively.

Additionally, creating feature references, case studies, and press releases for specific functionalities facilitates warm connection calls that existing customers are inclined to accept from potential prospects. There's no stronger endorsement than satisfied customers speaking positively about your product, a testament to the exceptional service provided by your CS teams. Establishing channels for existing customers to easily recommend your platform to their peers can significantly enhance your lead and opportunity pipeline.

Achieving revenue growth through customer success typically involves two different teams within Customer Success Organization. Firstly, there are account managers, often referred to as hunter-farmers, who are adept at filling quarterly quotas through value-driven relationship selling. Conversely, traditional success managers excel at driving adoption and mapping use cases, primarily focusing on organic sales strategies to increase revenue and attachment rates.

In my two decades of experience, I have observed that success managers with a knack for driving adoption and use case mapping are best suited for organic selling, leveraging their expertise to organically increase customer sales and revenue. On the other hand, account managers specialize in inorganic sales, adept at expanding product offerings to different business units and building relationships across various departments and geographical regions. Their ability to foster relationships opens doors for success managers to pitch and deliver value to auxiliary roles within customer organizations.

In conclusion, this chapter delves into the transformative concept of the customer flywheel, highlighting its pivotal phases and the critical role of the customer success team in revenue generation. We have explored the symbiotic relationship between customer satisfaction and business growth, uncovering actionable strategies across three key dimensions: organic revenue addition, inorganic revenue expansion, and the amplification of value through customer references.

By prioritizing customer satisfaction and fostering robust engagement, organizations can perpetuate a dynamic cycle of success, driving sustained revenue growth and enduring customer loyalty. The collaboration between account management and customer success teams emerges as a key driver in achieving tangible outcomes, leveraging their respective strengths to optimize sales strategies and enhance customer relationships.

Through a balanced approach encompassing organic and inorganic sales tactics, coupled with a focus on cultivating customer references, organizations can unlock the full potential of the customer flywheel, propelling their business towards sustained success in the competitive market landscape.

15

MASTERING METRICS: PATH TO SUCCESS EXCELLENCE

This chapter will highlight the key metrics that every successful leader should closely monitor. These metrics serve as important indicators of customer success and drive continuous improvement. CEOs and CFOs must integrate these metrics into the compensation structure of successful leaders to ensure alignment with organizational goals. Likewise, individual CSMs must understand how their contributions impact these critical metrics, driving efforts towards positive organizational outcomes.

Let us first explore essential customer success metrics. This section highlights two critical indicators: Gross Retention Rate (GRR) and Net Retention Rate (NRR). GRR measures the percentage of revenue retained from existing customers, while NRR considers revenue expansion and churn, providing a comprehensive view of revenue performance. In my experience, achieving a zero-churn rate is impossible unless you sell ice cream. However, minimizing churn is crucial for sustained business growth. Customer Success leaders play a pivotal role in reducing churn and driving revenue growth from existing customers, impacting the organization's financial health. Furthermore, leveraging Customer Success teams to generate additional revenue from existing customers is imperative. By prioritizing customer value and identifying additional revenue opportunities, Customer Success leaders significantly contribute to revenue expansion. In summary, the primary metrics for Customer Success leaders revolve around retaining existing revenue and driving additional revenue from the customer base, offering a comprehensive assessment of the effectiveness of Customer Success strategies organization-wide.

As you navigate through the layers of the customer success team down to the individual CSM, various other metrics come into play for which the CSM bears responsibility. Starting with NPS (Net Promoter Score), this metric offers valuable insight into whether customers are inclined to recommend your product or service to others. However, it's crucial not to focus solely on achieving the highest NPS score. Instead, emphasize NPS coverage, ensuring that CSMs gather feedback from all customers they engage with, regardless of the score obtained. Additionally, I advocate for the use of NPS as a leading indicator. This metric helps in understanding customer issues downstream, providing valuable insights even if a low NPS score is received. Ultimately, while NPS is an essential metric, it should not be the sole measure of a CSM's effectiveness in ensuring customer success.

Another key responsibility of CSMs is monitoring customer lifetime value (CLV) or the net revenue generated by each customer, tracking its growth on a monthly, quarterly, and yearly basis. This metric provides valuable insight into the overall value of the CSM's portfolio and serves as a positive indicator of their contribution to the company's finances and growth.

Furthermore, CSMs should focus on adoption and usage metrics, ensuring that customers are effectively utilizing and deriving maximum value from the product. It is essential for CSMs to take ownership of driving customer adoption via success plans, utilizing tools such as advanced analytics to gain insights into customer usage patterns. Implementing documented customer product and service entitlements and consumption plans and holding CSMs accountable for their execution is critical in ensuring customer satisfaction and long-term success.

Monitoring the movement of points of contact (POCs) or sponsors within and outside customer organizations is essential. CSMs should be incentivized to actively manage this by conducting Quarterly Business Reviews (QBRs) and other account management tasks. It's crucial to keep POC information regularly updated in Customer Success tools like Gainsight or Salesforce, providing senior leadership with real-time insights into each customer contact's status. Prioritizing this ensures organizations can maintain strong relationships and adapt to any changes within customer teams effectively. This is critical because if a promoter leaves a customer or if a competitor's advocate joins the customer in a position of influence, there could be revenue risk down the line.

Another important aspect that CSMs should be incentivized on is advocacy. Advocacy signifies the level of customer motivation and investment in your product, service, or platform, demonstrated by their willingness to speak positively about it on public platforms. There are various forms of advocacy, including press releases, case studies, blind references, and testimonials featured on websites or social media channels. Encouraging and fostering a culture of advocacy among customers is crucial, as it not only validates your product within the customer community but also indicates their satisfaction and value derived from it. This fosters a community of loyal customers who genuinely appreciate your product and are willing to promote it to others.

Next in line is account management, an integral part of the customer success organization. As we have previously discussed, these teams function as our hunter-farmer units, responsible for driving additional revenue from existing customers. In organizations where a dedicated account management team is absent, it is crucial to assign upsell targets to Customer Success Managers (CSMs). However, it is essential to ensure that CSM compensation is structured appropriately, focusing on incentivizing the right behaviors. It is imperative to avoid imposing sales targets on CSMs that detract from their primary role of nurturing and educating customers.

In organizations where CSMs are the primary drivers of leads from existing customers, their compensation structure should reflect a combination of fixed, variable, and bonus components. The fixed component ensures stability, while the variable component should be tied to key customer success metrics such as adoption, usage, advocacy, and churn reduction. Moreover, incentivizing CSMs with bonuses for successfully selling additional products or services to customers can further align their incentives with organizational goals. This approach ensures that CSMs focus on delivering value to customers first, with sales activities serving as an added bonus rather than a primary objective. However, if your organization has a dedicated account management team, it is crucial to prioritize key sales-related metrics for them. These metrics include quota attainment, pipeline contribution, and booking assistance. Their performance in achieving these numbers should determine the variable component of their compensation.

The next team I would like to address is the professional services team, encompassing various functions such as implementation, technical solutions, and business consulting. When building your professional services team, it is essential to focus on key metrics, the most critical being time to value. Time to value is indeed crucial, comprising two key metrics: the speed at which the implementation team can onboard the customer and ensure their effective product utilization. While some organizations also prioritize booking-to-billing cycles as a vital metric, it is essential to recognize that this metric is not exclusive to implementation goals. It encompasses multiple teams and factors, including contract structures and sales team contributions. Another important metric to consider is the percentage of projects delivered on time. Timely delivery is critical for ensuring customers go live promptly. Assessing performance based on whether delivery times are below or above average can help determine variable or compensation structures for professional services leadership.

The next crucial metric to consider is customer satisfaction. However, it is important to recognize that the professional services team operates differently from the tech support team, as their interactions with customers typically have a longer duration. In my experience, engagements with the professional services team tend to be transactional— they involve one-time activities with customers, after which the team moves on to the next project or customer.

As a successful leader, it is essential to focus on measuring transactional engagements in terms of customer satisfaction surveys. After your team disengages from a project, it is vital to gather feedback from the customer through satisfaction surveys. Analyzing these scores and incorporating them into the variable or compensation structure for the professional services team can help ensure continuous improvement and alignment with customer needs.

In a professional services organization, one of the most pivotal metrics to track is utilization. Its significance spans two crucial dimensions. Firstly, it encompasses resource utilization, but equally important is its role as a metric for assessing the profitability of service teams. Utilization can be dissected into two main components: billable utilization and resource utilization. Extensive literature exists on measuring utilization effectively, illuminating its dual role in evaluating both the financial performance and operational efficiency of deployed teams.

Following closely in importance is another key metric: project margins and profitability. Ultimately, the primary objective for any professional services leader is to drive revenue and maximize profits for stakeholders. This involves meticulously analyzing the costs associated with resources such as personnel, technology, and travel and contrasting them against the revenue generated. The resulting profit margin and overall profitability serve as critical indicators of success. Just as with utilization, there is an abundance of literature and metrics available to guide professionals in maximizing profitability within the realm of professional services.

Let us explore the key metrics for technical support or support organizations dealing with tactical customer issues. One essential metric is the Service Level Agreement (SLA), which measures the time taken to resolve specific customer problems. Typically, this is expressed as a percentage attainment, indicating the proportion of cases resolved within the agreed-upon timeframe. Another important metric is the average handling time, which measures how long it takes to address customer issues. Optimizing this metric involves streamlining processes to reduce wait times and improve overall efficiency, enhancing customer satisfaction.

Another crucial metric for assessing your support team's performance is the quality score. This score reflects deviations from established standard practices regarding case handling, measurement, communication, debugging, and resolution. Implementing and applying various quality standards is essential in this regard. However, to mitigate self-selection bias, it's advisable to have a third-party or independent team evaluate performance quality, ensuring unbiased assessment.

Next, let us address Agent Productivity, a vital measure of your agents' efficiency. Tracking metrics such as the number of tickets resolved daily or the average number of tickets handled per agent within a given timeframe can provide valuable insights. Every tech support leader should prioritize improving this metric to gauge team productivity effectively. Customer satisfaction follows closely in importance to the service level agreement (SLA). Measured through metrics like CSAT, it provides invaluable feedback on the quality of support provided.

The support function operates as a transactional team, where integrating customer satisfaction surveys into the post-resolution process is crucial. Beyond overall customer satisfaction, it's also vital to measure the survey return rate. This metric goes beyond simply assessing the CSAT score an agent receives; it evaluates how frequently customers engage with the survey process. Although this metric isn't directly within the support agent's control, it's essential for understanding customer sentiment and improving service quality.

Driving up the service return survey rate is crucial. Strategies to achieve this include having agents remind customers to complete the survey, emphasizing its importance in enhancing service quality. In my experience, this approach has proven effective, as customers understand the significance of their feedback in refining service levels. Therefore, aim to achieve a service return rate of 25 to 30 percent, as this indicates robust engagement and a positive response to your service efforts.

Another important metric to consider is customer touchpoints, which refers to the number of interactions the team has with a customer before resolving a case. It is evident that the more engagements required before issue resolution, the poorer the overall customer experience. To enhance customer satisfaction, it is essential to optimize this metric by minimizing the number of touchpoints needed to resolve a case. Companies often track first call resolution (FCR) and first contact resolution (FCR) as additional metrics. These metrics measure the percentage of cases resolved with only one interaction with the customer, aiming to keep this percentage as high as possible to streamline the support process.

Lastly, the escalation rate is a key metric to measure. This metric evaluates the percentage of cases where the customer escalates the issue due to dissatisfaction with the resolution, delay in resolution process, follow-up questions, or unresolved cases. It is imperative to keep the escalation rate to a minimum to ensure effective issue resolution and customer satisfaction. These are essential metrics for every customer experience (CX) leader to consider to improve support processes and continuously enhance overall customer satisfaction.

In conclusion, this comprehensive exploration underscores the importance of key metrics in guiding the success of customer-centric organizational functions. From tracking revenue retention and expansion to ensuring efficient issue resolution and maximizing customer satisfaction, these metrics are essential indicators of organizational health and performance.

As leaders, it is crucial to integrate these metrics into compensation structures, thereby aligning incentives with strategic objectives and driving continuous improvement initiatives. By doing so, organizations can ensure that every customer success team member, from executives to individual contributors, is motivated and empowered to prioritize customer needs and deliver exceptional experiences.

Navigating through the intricate layers of customer success teams, understanding and leveraging these metrics enable leaders to make informed decisions, identify areas for improvement, and ultimately drive sustained business growth. Embracing a data-driven approach and fostering a culture of accountability around these metrics will be instrumental in propelling organizations towards their long-term success and customer satisfaction goals.

16

THE ART OF DRIVING SUCCESS THROUGH ENABLEMENT

Customer Success Enablement stands as a cornerstone within any customer success organization. As leaders embark on establishing a dedicated customer success team, prioritizing the planning and scaling of enablement initiatives becomes paramount. Let us explore the critical elements that demand attention when setting up the Customer Success enablement function.

First and foremost, it is imperative to identify the unique needs of the customer success team. As discussed in previous chapters, every customer success team operates differently. Some focus primarily on account management, while others delve into technical aspects and implementation. Understanding these distinctions is crucial in tailoring enablement efforts to meet specific team requirements.

When building a customer success team, it is imperative to prioritize Customer Success Enablement. The most important aspect of the enablement plan is developing a robust onboarding structure. This involves comprehending the lifecycle of a customer success manager (CSM) within your organization. What skills are readily available in the market, and what unique skills does your organization demand? Consider the persona of a CSM on their first day. What facets of customer success, such as success operations, portfolio reviews, and QBRs, should they be acquainted with? While certain aspects of customer success and technical skills may be readily accessible, each successful organization has distinct requirements. Some skills cannot be hired but must be instilled in CSMs upon entering the organization. As a CS leader, it is vital to understand the needs of a CSM throughout each phase of their tenure, from zero to three months, three to six months, six to 12 months, and beyond. I firmly advocate for ongoing customer ever-boarding, ensuring that CSMs receive continuous training and development. Therefore, establishing a structured enablement and onboarding framework for success managers is paramount.

Another critical consideration is role-based training, given the diverse teams within a customer success organization, encompassing tech support, account management, and field teams focused on upsells. Tailoring dedicated training modules to each role facilitates a more effective learning path, potentially organized into levels or courses with corresponding certifications. Moreover, personalized training is essential, particularly for smaller teams seeking to maximize the potential of each CSM. This entails identifying skill, training, and knowledge gaps during the interview process and implementing a personalized learning plan. Just as with customers, the initial 90 days of a CSM's tenure in your organization are crucial, highlighting the significance of a personalized training regimen.

The third aspect to consider is product knowledge. As we have discussed, every CS leader understands that each organization is unique, and certain aspects of training are specific to your organization. Product and technical stack knowledge are essential for a CSM, but unfortunately, it is challenging to find in the market. It is difficult to hire someone who comprehends how a particular product functions. Therefore, collaboration with product leaders is essential to develop robust training and enablement programs focused on product knowledge for your CSMs.

Additionally, CS leaders should approach enablement in a modular fashion, creating content and training materials that can be repurposed for customer onboarding. For instance, each aspect can be developed into separate training modules to educate individuals on product functionality, configuration, and maximizing ROI. These modules can then be utilized for both internal CSM training and customer education.

In the following section of this chapter, let us go through the significance of soft skills. Often overlooked yet immensely valuable, soft skills are crucial for the onboarding and training of CSMs. They represent essential competencies and the cornerstone of a successful CSM's repertoire. Like any customer-facing role, mastering soft skills is indispensable for CSM effectiveness. These soft skills encompass a broad spectrum, including active listening, empathy, communication, and problem-solving. Integrating these criteria into the CSM evaluation process during recruitment ensures a well-rounded team. Continuous evaluation and training across these metrics are essential for ongoing improvement. Three key aspects that greatly impact a CSM's career are soft skills, effective communication, and the ability to articulate the needs of both the company and the customer. Clear and timely communication with customers and internal stakeholders underscores the importance of effective soft skills development within the CSM role.

Another critical soft skill for every CSM is handling difficult customers. While I strongly advocate for prioritizing customer needs, there are times when guidance is essential to guide them appropriately. CSMs must ensure that even irate customers feel heard and valued, placing their needs above organizational goals during interactions. It is essential for CSMs to effectively manage challenging, frustrated customers, a skill that requires continuous refinement and development.

Moreover, CSMs should be able to identify opportunities for cross-selling and upselling, even though specialized account managers usually handle these tasks. Offering training on recognizing such opportunities and effectively communicating the value of your product is crucial. While not traditionally part of a CSM's role, organizations should equip their CSMs with the necessary skills for cross-selling and upselling. Additionally, it is essential to train CSMs in basic technology and soft skills to understand customer personas, including the prevalent concept of Ideal Customer Persona (ICP) in the industry. This foundational knowledge enhances their ability to tailor interactions and solutions to meet individual customer needs effectively.

CSMs, like your sales team, should have a profound understanding of the diverse customer personas within the organization, including their unique requirements and priorities. This insight enables CSMs to tailor their training approach effectively, optimizing outcomes for your company. Additionally, it is crucial for organizations to develop a comprehensive customer journey map if they still need to do so. This map delineates where customers should ideally reside in their life cycle regarding spending, usage, and exposure to various product features. Every CSM should be well-versed in this map to understand the expected levels of product usage and comprehension at different stages.

Moreover, CSMs should have a firm grasp of your organization's corporate pitch, mission, vision, and core values. At a minimum, they should be capable of delivering a basic product demo. Another essential skill for a customer success manager is analytics proficiency. This skill enables them to either analyze provided data or utilize basic analytic tools like Power BI or Tableau to comprehend various metrics, track costs, identify trends, and make informed, data-driven decisions for timely interventions.

Another critical aspect that customer success leaders should grasp is the importance of regular training updates to keep their team abreast of industry regulations, policies, and governance changes. This ensures timely responses to evolving regulatory landscapes and international market dynamics relevant to their customers. Business acumen is vital for CSMs to navigate customer interactions effectively in the real market.

Before a CSM starts interacting with customers and key stakeholders, several preparatory steps are crucial. Firstly, shadowing plays a pivotal role. New CSMs should shadow experienced counterparts to grasp the organization's unique processes, including how to handle tech support cases and analyze customer usage data. The duration of shadowing varies based on the complexity of the product and customer use cases, typically lasting one to four weeks. This preparatory phase is vital before CSMs transition to independent customer interactions. Additionally, real-world scenario simulations, like Farmers Market QBRs or issue resolution walkthroughs, offer invaluable experiential learning opportunities, enabling CSMs better to understand their role and the organization's operations. Roleplay is another invaluable aspect to consider. In my experience, mock QBRs have been instrumental in differentiating exceptional CSMs from average ones during the interview process. Roleplay sessions are essential for ensuring your CSMs are well-prepared to engage with customer stakeholders.

Furthermore, certification programs play a crucial role. CSMs should independently review program content and complete evaluations to earn certification. These certifications offer several benefits. Firstly, they instill confidence in CSMs, validating their expertise. Secondly, they extend to other members associated with your organization, such as partner success managers, fostering a common understanding of your product and use cases. Moreover, certifications reassure customers that their CSMs are knowledgeable and competent, alleviating concerns for key stakeholders.

The final component of continuous enablement involves cross-functional collaboration. Inward-looking enablement programs often need to be updated and grasp the broader organizational context. When designing a training plan for customer success managers (CSMs), it is crucial to gather input from within the customer success team and key stakeholders across departments like sales, engineering, and product. Representatives from each of these functions should contribute to CSM enablement, ensuring that CSMs are up-to-date with the latest developments and have access to points of contact within each function to assist them in real-world scenarios. For instance, I ensure that product leaders provide training to CSMs in my team, enabling them to effectively address product-related issues or customer requests.

Feedback is another vital aspect, serving as a pivotal tool in assessing the effectiveness of the enablement program and making necessary adjustments to ensure it achieves its objectives. The primary stakeholders for feedback are the CSMs who have completed the training. It is essential to gather feedback from them immediately after they finish the coursework and again six weeks after starting their role. The initial feedback offers insights into the mechanics of training delivery, while the feedback after six weeks evaluates how well the training has been applied in real-world scenarios. Customer Success Managers should provide feedback on their training experience immediately after completion and after six weeks of implementation.

Another key stakeholder to seek feedback from is the customer's point of contact (POC). It is essential to inquire whether the CSM appears trained, enabled, and knowledgeable during interactions. This conversation requires sensitivity to avoid undermining the CSM's credibility while genuinely seeking input on their preparedness. Based on my experience, seeking customer feedback immediately after a CSM is assigned may not yield accurate insights due to various parameters influencing the assessment during the initial weeks. Therefore, feedback from existing customers who have had the CSM for at least six months provides a more reliable gauge of training effectiveness. This feedback loop ensures that CSMs receive the necessary training and support to excel in their roles, facilitating continuous improvement in the enablement process.

Another critical source of feedback on CSM training comes from CSM counterparts, such as sales representatives, implementation managers, or executives who interact closely with CSMs and assess their performance. Continuously seeking feedback from these stakeholders is essential to ensure ongoing improvement. It is crucial to close the loop on feedback by implementing changes to the enablement program based on the insights gathered.

A major obstacle in CSM enablement is addressing tribal knowledge, where individuals hoard information. Cultivating a culture of collaboration and knowledge-sharing is crucial to ensure that essential information is distributed efficiently, enabling CSMs to access the necessary resources promptly and excel in their roles. Establishing a platform for sharing knowledge and fostering a culture of collaboration from leadership down can dismantle silos and foster teamwork among team members.

Establishing channels where no question is considered "bad" and creating a safe environment for CSMs to ask questions freely can encourage knowledge-sharing. When leaders, including the CEO, actively engage in addressing queries, it sets a tone for a culture of sharing and support. Additionally, developing standard operating procedures (SOPs) ensures consistency and clarity in organizational processes. Documenting these procedures and ensuring accessibility for all team members, irrespective of tenure, is essential for fostering effective knowledge-sharing and collaboration. Thus, establishing and documenting SOPs are crucial in promoting knowledge-sharing and efficiency within the organization.

Regular workshops and training sessions should be integral to your organization, providing platforms for senior CSMs to share their insights and best practices with everyone. Celebrating these knowledge-sharing sessions is essential, recognizing senior CSMs' contributions and rewarding them for their efforts. This fosters a culture of open information exchange and encourages ongoing participation.

Moreover, monitoring and acknowledging these efforts to maintain active participation from senior CSMs is crucial. Investing in essential tools like customer relationship management, customer success management, analytics, and learning management systems can streamline knowledge-sharing and enablement processes. Although these tools may seem separate, comprehensive solutions like Gainsight or Salesforce integrate these functionalities seamlessly. Despite the initial investment, these platforms provide accessible information and documentation to all team members, fostering equal access and collaboration. Embracing these best practices in customer success enablement enables organizations to enhance the overall customer experience, leading to increased satisfaction, loyalty, and revenue growth.

In conclusion, Customer Success Enablement is a cornerstone of any customer success organization. As leaders establish dedicated customer success teams, prioritizing the planning and scaling of enablement initiatives becomes paramount. Critical elements include identifying unique team needs, establishing robust onboarding structures, tailoring training to roles, fostering soft skills development, and equipping CSMs with product knowledge and cross-functional collaboration skills. Feedback loops and addressing tribal knowledge are crucial for ongoing improvement. By embracing these best practices, organizations can enhance the overall customer experience, driving satisfaction, loyalty, and revenue growth.

17

INTERVIEW: BEING CUSTOMER FIRST FROM DAY 1

Guest: Raviteja Dodda, Co-founder and CEO, MoEngage

Introduction

Ravi: Raviteja (Ravi) Dodda is the Co-founder and CEO of MoEngage, an insights-led customer engagement platform built for customer-obsessed marketers and product owners. He is an alumnus of IIT-Kharagpur. Ravi has over 10 years of experience leading global teams and managing successful products. Prior to MoEngage, he co-founded and built DelightCircle, a local-offers mobile app. Ravi has been recognized in the BW Disrupt 40 under 40 and Forbes 30 under 30 lists.

MoEngage: MoEngage is an insights-led customer engagement platform trusted by over 1,200 global consumer brands such as Ally

Financial, McAfee, Flipkart, Domino's, Nestle, Deutsche Telekom, OYO, and more. MoEngage empowers marketers and product owners with insights into customer behavior and the ability to act on those insights to engage customers across the web, mobile, email, social, and messaging channels. Consumer brands in 59 countries use MoEngage to power digital experiences for over a billion monthly customers. With offices in 13 countries, MoEngage is backed by Goldman Sachs Asset Management, B Capital, Steadview Capital, Multiples Private Equity, Eight Roads, F-Prime Capital, Matrix Partners, Ventureast, and Helion Ventures. MoEngage was named a Strong Performer in The Forrester Wave™ 2023 reports and the Leader in the IDC MarketScape: Worldwide Omni-Channel Marketing Platforms for B2C Enterprises 2023.

Atma: I express my gratitude to you, Ravi, for taking the time to participate in this discussion. Let's kick off by delving into "What Customer Success means to you?"

Ravi: From my perspective, customer success revolves around assisting customers in attaining their desired outcomes and ensuring they achieve their business goals. In our specific case, for example, consumer brands aim to enhance customer lifetime value, boost retention rates, and increase conversions with their end users through enhanced engagement. Thus, the role of our customer success managers or customer success team is to support our clients in reaching the objectives they set out to achieve using our platform. Our ultimate objective is to exceed customer expectations while enabling them to achieve their desired results, thus fostering strong advocacy. It's crucial to acknowledge that customer success is not solely the responsibility of one department; rather, it is a collective obligation of our entire organization.

Atma: That perspective is indeed well presented, Ravi. It is worth noting that you have achieved remarkable success as one of the youngest CEOs in the industry. When you initially embarked on your journey, you had limited experience in the B2B SAAS domain. I'm curious to learn about the steps you took to acquire the necessary knowledge in this field. Furthermore, it is evident that you prioritized customer success as a pivotal aspect of your management and leadership strategy right from the beginning. Could you elaborate on how you approached and implemented customer success strategies as a young CEO?

Ravi: That's a great question, Atma. When I founded the company in 2014, I had limited experience in running a SAAS company. As a result, we found ourselves encountering some challenges in terms of unfamiliar terminology and processes. It also meant that we made our fair share of mistakes and had to reinvent the wheel at times. Also, over the past decade, the customer success function has evolved significantly, and customers have become more mature in their expectations.

In the early days, it was instinctive for us to prioritize delivering value to our customers to ensure sustained success. For the first four years of the company, from 2014 until 2018, a significant portion of our growth was driven by word-of-mouth referrals fueled by a strong customer success DNA. Looking back, we now realize that we could have done better in terms of marketing during those initial years.

It also helped that the ecosystem was relatively small. When people moved from one company to another, we found that as long as we provided exceptional service to our customers, positive word-of-mouth would naturally follow. So, to some extent, it was a natural progression for us. We initially observed how others handled Customer Success, and we began researching and educating ourselves on metrics that mattered. We gained valuable insights by consuming online content, which helped us define our approach.

Overall, it has been a journey of continuous learning and refining our customer success strategies to meet the evolving needs of our clients.

Atma: Thank you, Ravi, for sharing your insights. It's truly impressive to see your modesty, though I must say that your natural inclination towards customer success is evident. It was, in fact, one of the primary reasons that attracted me to MoEngage, witnessing the level of importance you place on ensuring customer success. It is one thing to be aware of the investment required in customer success is one thing, but effectively convincing investors and other functions within the organization is a different challenge altogether. I'm curious to learn more about your process for setting up a customer success function. How do you navigate this process and successfully establish customer success as a valued and integral part of our company?

Ravi: The process of setting up a customer success (CS) function can vary depending on the scale of the company. In the initial stages, when the customer base is small (around five to ten customers), the approach will be different. Constraints on hiring and the types of roles needed will dictate the strategy. Initially, it may require individuals who can wear multiple hats and be hands-on. For example, one person might handle technical support, customer success, value realization, and writing best practices - demonstrating a high level of learnability and adaptability.

As the company grows and progresses beyond this initial phase, specialization becomes necessary. A leader can be hired to oversee the CS function, and roles can be more clearly defined. Measurement becomes crucial, with retention and leading indicators like Net Promoter Score (NPS) taking center stage. Both leading and trailing indicators should receive equal attention to understand the impact of CS on business outcomes. This may require hiring an experienced leader with a proven track record in scaling portfolios and working towards segmentation.

At higher growth stages (e.g., $10 million-plus business), the separation between Customer onboarding (product implementation), Customer Success (ongoing value realization) and Transactional Product Support become more pronounced. Additionally, based on customer value and scale investment in digital experiences and determining the level of touch required (low touch versus high touch) becomes crucial. Instead of focusing solely on reducing churn, shifting your focus towards building satisfied customers and avoiding potential issues with problem accounts is very critical at this stage of the company.

In conclusion, the process of setting up a CS function evolves as the company grows, encompassing specialization, measurement, segmentation, and a customer-centric approach based on the company's scale and customer success.

Atma: That's an excellent observation, Ravi. While CEOs have access to the same literature on metrics and KPIs, your focus on NPS, happiness quotient, and value deliverability truly sets you apart. It's commendable and a crucial aspect that young CEOs should learn from. Additionally, I appreciate your insights on the parameters considered when hiring leaders.

Moving on, one of the key challenges CEOs, especially in the current market, face is the active selling and positioning of Customer Success. It's not alway easy for CEOs or go-to-market teams to convey the value and sell it effectively. I'm interested to understand your thoughts on this matter. How do you approach the positioning of Customer Success? Do you perceive it as a profit center or a cost center?

Ravi: Certainly! Positioning and pricing Customer Success can vary based on geographical locations and company size. When reaching a decent scale, typically around five million in ARR or more, it becomes advisable to incorporate pricing for implementation, customer success, and support as separate line items. This approach is commonly seen in the US and European markets, particularly with mid-market and enterprise customers. In such cases, negotiations are less likely to occur for these specific line items. Enterprises often recognize the costs associated with implementing software and that it may require dedicated resources for successful adoption.

Although challenges may arise in the Asian market, it is still beneficial to proactively include these costs in the pricing structure. By doing so, it facilitates the organization's ability to invest in and demonstrate the importance of Customer Success. It is crucial to consider the specific nature of the product and the market when determining how to position and price Customer Success as either a profit center or a cost center.

Atma: Considering the current economy, the pressure on profitability, and market trends, how do you perceive the role of Customer Success evolving compared to its state five to ten years ago?

Ravi: In the evolving landscape of customer success, it has become increasingly important for companies to demonstrate the value of their products or services, particularly in the SAAS industry. Without showcasing value, companies may face cost-cutting pressures. To address this, the role of Customer Success Managers (CSMs) has become crucial. Engagement Managers and CSMs need to bring together various teams such as technical support and product engineering to cater to customers' needs effectively. Understanding the customers' environment and business requirements, combined with expertise in the SAAS product domain, allows CSMs to offer best practices and become trusted partners.

Regarding the cost structure of the Customer Success (CS) function, SAAS company CEOs should consider monetizing CS services based on a clear cost and value aspect. It is also important to establish benchmarks to determine the appropriate percentage of revenue that should be allocated to CS costs. These benchmarks can be derived from models that consider the desired gross margins for SAAS companies. CEOs are not averse to investing in CS; they simply want to ensure that the company maintains the right unit economics, including gross margins, sales, and marketing expenses.

Constraints can prompt companies to think differently and find innovative approaches to problem-solving. For instance, investing in digital CS or optimizing CS operations can allow companies to allocate more time to customers at different maturity levels. Determining the balance between high-touch, low-touch, and self-serve approaches depends on the specific needs of the product and its target market. Providing templates and easy onboarding processes can enable customers to quickly derive value from the product.

Adversities, in a way, can be beneficial as they encourage companies to adapt and find alternative solutions. Looking ahead, these changing dynamics are likely to shape the next decade, leading to the creation of more profitable companies with a focus on customer success!

Atma: Indeed, a profitable company benefits all stakeholders, including investors, employees, and customers. This aligns great with the next topic I had for you around the trends we observe in the market: Customer Success as a revenue center.

This extends beyond selling Customer Success (CS) as a standalone product and delves into leveraging it as a means to drive upselling and cross-selling opportunities.

I'm curious to hear your perspective on this matter. How do you view the potential of Customer Success in generating additional revenue, and where do you see this trend heading in the future?

Ravi: Absolutely, as companies evolve and expand, and customer acquisition costs continue to rise and leveraging Customer Success becomes even more critical. Especially in the case of multi-product companies, there is an opportunity to build on existing customer segments. By having a well-established Customer Success (CS) function that works in tandem with management and sales, companies can effectively introduce additional products and modules that cater to specific customer needs. This not only enhances the customer life time value by ensuring customer happiness and advocacy but also provides an avenue to educate customers on new use cases and expand their business goals using the company's new products.

Customer Success can play a vital role in creating a demand for these new products and generating expansion opportunities. By understanding customers' needs and aligning them with the benefits of the new offerings, CS can drive adoption and demonstrate the value to customers. This expansion strategy ultimately has a direct impact on the metrics of the sales function, as it creates new opportunities for upselling and cross-selling.

As companies continue to evolve and introduce new products, CS will play a significant role in driving revenue growth and shaping the overall success of the organization. By leveraging the expertise and relationships cultivated through the CS function, companies can unlock the full potential of their customer base and drive profitable expansion.

Atma: Thank you, Ravi. I have one final question for you, and it revolves around your expertise in building a culture of customer success within an organization. If you were to provide advice to young CEOs on how they can establish and foster a strong culture of customer success, similar to what you have accomplished, what key message or advice would you impart?

Ravi: Creating a culture of customer success begins with the people within the organization. It is crucial to ensure that leaders, regardless of their role in engineering, sales, or marketing, embrace a customer-obsessed mindset. This means they prioritize the customer's needs and avoid acquiring customers who may not be the best fit for the company's offerings.

Similarly, the product team should also adopt a customer-obsessed approach. They should go beyond simply building products and consider the customer's value and happiness as key factors. To establish this culture, it is essential to hire individuals who already possess this mindset or educate and align existing team members. Leaders must be fully committed to and believe in creating a customer-centric culture. Once leaders are onboard, they can drive this culture downwards, from product leaders to product managers and engineering leaders.

Building a customer success culture is not an instantaneous process. It requires consistent reinforcement on every forum and constant e mphasis. Additionally, leading by example plays a significant role. Leaders need to demonstrate their commitment by actively engaging with customers, jumping on calls, and addressing real customer problems. When leaders exemplify this behavior, the rest of the team follows suit.

Ultimately, creating a culture of customer success relies on the collective effort of leaders and team members across the organization. By prioritizing the customer, aligning mindsets, and leading by example, a strong customer success culture can be nurtured and ingrained, benefiting the organization as a whole.

Atma: Thank you, Ravi, for sharing your valuable insights and expertise. Your perspectives have been incredibly insightful and will undoubtedly inspire and benefit my readers. Your time and contributions are greatly appreciated.

18

PART IV: FUTURE

In the final section, "Customer Success in Uncertain Markets," I offer essential strategies for CSMs to navigate turbulent markets effectively, emphasizing mastering fundamentals amidst uncertainty using the PRESS method — Proactive monitoring, Revenue Focus, Efficiency optimization, Scalability, and Stickiness.

Proactiveness involves vigilantly monitoring usage trends and understanding macroeconomic factors. Revenue Focus demands a deep dive into customers' financial metrics, painting a vivid picture of value creation. Efficiency optimization prioritizes investments in training and automation, streamlining operations with precision. Scalability involves orchestrating resources effectively and creating a dynamic canvas of growth potential. Stickiness emphasizes building enduring customer relationships, adding vibrant hues to the customer success palette.

In the subsequent chapter, "Future of The Success Manager Role," we cover the evolving landscape of the CSM role in B2B SaaS, where vibrant shifts are underway. Traditional responsibilities transform as product-led growth strategies infuse energy into platform adoption efforts. Key profiles, like account managers, operational managers, and subject matter experts, bring their expertise to the canvas of customer success. Adaptability and ongoing skill development are essential for navigating this ever-changing landscape, where CSM roles transition to digital teams and specialized expertise, adding splashes of color to the canvas of success.

19

CUSTOMER SUCCESS IN UNCERTAIN MARKETS

In this chapter, my goal is to offer additional context and insights on how Customer Success Managers (CSMs) can effectively navigate turbulent markets and position themselves as adept platformers. Drawing from my experiences throughout my career, which include navigating through significant challenges such as the 2008 and 2010 subprime crisis, as well as the COVID-related restrictions from 2020 to 2022 and the subsequent post-COVID financial downturn,

I understand the importance of mastering the fundamentals. In the ever-changing market landscape, it is essential for CSMs to not only survive but thrive. Within these pages, I share valuable tricks and best practices essential for CSMs to excel amidst turbulent market conditions.

One crucial advice I offer is to gain insight into the market and macroeconomic factors that influence your customer's business. Whether you specialize in a specific industry or work as a generalist

CSM, comprehending these variables is essential. For instance, consider the ramifications of funding challenges for your customers. How do they affect operations and vendor payment capabilities? What strategies can they employ to mitigate currency risks? To address these challenges, I have developed a strategy called PRESS: Proactive, Revenue Focus, Efficiency, Scale, and Stickiness. Throughout this chapter, I'll cover each aspect of PRESS and offer actionable guidance for CSMs seeking to excel in turbulent markets. These strategies are essential for CSMs to effectively navigate uncertain market conditions.

Regarding proactiveness, it is imperative for every Customer Success (CS) team member to consistently monitor usage, billing, and key contact movements across all accounts in their portfolio. This practice is fundamental for every CSM, regardless of macroeconomic conditions—it is akin to basic CS hygiene. However, it is now critical to go beyond merely tracking these trends and to connect them to the broader context. For instance, if you observe several high-level executives departing from your customer's company, it serves as a significant red flag. Similarly, if compliance-related issues persistently arise on your customer's behalf, that's another cause for concern. Therefore, analyzing these metrics and correlating them with the larger business landscape is essential.

Understanding how your customer perceives their business is paramount. Are they primarily focused on B2B or B2C markets? Which regions are they aiming to expand into, and are there any regions where they intend to scale back operations? How do they approach acquisitions— are they looking to acquire other companies, or are they being targeted for acquisition themselves? What are their primary monetization strategies in cases where they lack a stable revenue stream? Additionally, what major business pivots are they contemplating in the coming years? Mass layoffs or the departure of key executives should be considered red flags that warrant further investigation.

Moreover, it is essential for CSMs to monitor how customers utilize their own technical teams proactively. Are these teams dedicated to enhancing competitive value for the customer, or are they focused on developing tools and services that might replace your company's offerings? If the latter scenario is apparent, educating the customer on the differences between internal development and external procurement is crucial. Additionally, it offers insights into both approaches' key advantages and disadvantages to empower them to make well-informed decisions.

The next crucial aspect is Revenue Focus. It is imperative to understand your customers' bottom and top lines and how they contribute to them. Comprehensive comprehension of the commercial aspects of your customer is a key differentiator for success. As a CSM, understanding your company's contract with the customer is paramount. This entails grasping your costs to service the customer, the revenue generated from their business, and the resulting margins. Delving into the customer's breakdown in billing, including line items and billing lifecycles, offers insights into potential changes in future revenue streams.

Another critical aspect of Revenue Focus is understanding the value you bring to your customers. What return on investment (ROI) are you delivering? What revenue attribution does the customer associate with your company? Are you impacting their cost centers or profit centers? For instance, if you provide robotics automation, you might reduce service costs, whereas a sales efficiency tool might increase their revenue. Each offering has different impacts depending on various macro and microeconomic factors. Understanding these dynamics is essential for effectively demonstrating the value proposition to your customers.

Furthermore, consider whether you are replacing any workforce or creating additional cost-effectiveness for the customer. Are you enabling them to operate with fewer hires, or are you enhancing their teams' efficiency, thus potentially reducing the need for additional hires? Understanding these revenue advantages enables efficient value selling. CSMs should be the most revenue-savvy employees in the company, particularly during turbulent times, as they serve as gatekeepers of recurring revenue. Therefore, mastering revenue focus is vital for their success.

The third aspect is efficiency. During uncertain or financial macroeconomic distress, prioritizing efficiency becomes paramount for every CSM. As leaders and companies, these are the moments when investments in training and automation become crucial. While it might seem counterintuitive to focus on anything other than top-line and bottom-line impact during distress, it is necessary to recognize the long-term value-adds of such investments. Therefore, investing in automation and enablement as a CS leader is imperative.

Enhanced collaboration across teams— whether in engineering, product development, or sales— is crucial for optimizing efficiency and reducing errors. Support engineering teams, in particular, should aim to handle a higher volume of cases per day efficiently. Similarly, CSMs should focus on supporting more customers or generating increased revenue per person. This dedication to efficiency should be consistently applied throughout the entire process. CSMs should prioritize ongoing upskilling, reskilling, and exploration of new tools such as chatbots, generative AI, or other innovative technologies to streamline daily operations and enhance efficiency. Adaptability and a commitment to continuous improvement are indispensable for maximizing efficiency and successfully navigating turbulent times.

Next in the PRESS framework is Scalability. This involves recognizing opportunities as a customer success leader to effectively serve as many customers as possible with limited resources. Strategies for achieving scalability may include implementing diverse programs, establishing scalable teams, or integrating digital customer success management tools. By closely monitoring these initiatives, you can implement training or best practice coaching without the necessity of hiring additional CSMs, thereby leveraging existing resources to reach a broader customer base.

The final aspect of the PRESS framework is Stickiness, which is particularly crucial during turbulent times. We must excel at cultivating stronger bonds with our customers across all fronts. This involves creating stickiness around various use cases—the more use cases a customer can implement, the better. Similarly, the more features they utilize within our product, the stronger the connection becomes.

When considering stickiness, it is vital to map key customer contacts. Establishing stickiness and multithreading across the board ensures connectivity from Proof of Concept (POC) to decision-makers, executives, and customer representatives. Encouraging customers to engage more frequently with your platform and team is essential. Additionally, it is invaluable to have deeply entrenched customers whose success directly correlates with our product's impact on their bottom line and top line. These strategies must remain relevant and consistently applied, especially during turbulent times.

In this comprehensive chapter, I have provided invaluable insights and strategies for Customer Success Managers (CSMs) to navigate turbulent markets successfully. Drawing from my extensive experience, including navigating through significant crises like the 2008 and 2010 subprime crises and the recent COVID-related challenges, I emphasize the importance of mastering the fundamentals.

Key strategies discussed include gaining insight into market and macroeconomic factors impacting customers, prioritizing revenue focus, enhancing efficiency through training and automation, fostering collaboration across teams, and continuously upskilling. These strategies are vital for CSMs to excel amidst uncertainty and drive long-term success.

The PRESS framework, encompassing Proactiveness, Revenue Focus, Efficiency, Scalability, and Stickiness, serves as a guiding principle for effectively navigating turbulent times. Proactiveness ensures proactive monitoring and adaptation, while Revenue Focus emphasizes understanding customer value and optimizing revenue. Efficiency involves maximizing resources and streamlining operations, while Scalability focuses on efficiently serving a broader customer base.

Finally, Stickiness underscores the importance of fostering strong, lasting bonds with customers across all touchpoints. By implementing these strategies and embracing a commitment to continuous improvement, CSMs can weather turbulent times and emerge stronger and more resilient, ensuring sustained success for both themselves and their customers.

20

FUTURE OF THE SUCCESS MANAGER ROLE

In the dynamic world of B2B SaaS, where the primary focus is boosting adoption and usage, as a Customer Success Manager (CSM), it is crucial to remain alert to the changing landscape. While this viewpoint may not be widely shared, it is grounded in market trends, the necessity of profitability, and my direct experience witnessing the ongoing evolution of the CSM role. I anticipate an impending shift in the conventional duties of CSMs. However, if you are involved in a scale-up or startup striving to pinpoint a product-market fit in a particular region, there is little need for worry.

This chapter explores established B2B SaaS companies, where the traditional role of the Customer Success Manager (CSM) has long revolved around facilitating customer adoption and usage. However, this role is now evolving. The responsibility for driving platform adoption within customer organizations is shifting to the product team, which employs product-led growth strategies. This shift ensures that customers receive continuous updates about new features and are actively encouraged to adopt them.

These product-led growth strategies often harness automation programs and scalable communication channels to ensure customers adeptly utilize the platform to its fullest potential on a large scale. Furthermore, it is increasingly apparent that if CSMs predominantly manage technical support escalations and product performance issues, their roles will likely transition to tech support teams, commonly outsourced resources with lower monetary value. In areas with higher operational costs, the demand for traditional CSMs simply coordinating with technical support teams is dwindling. These duties will gradually shift towards support management. In this evolving landscape, customer success organizations must adapt accordingly. They are neglecting to do so and risk falling behind in the swiftly changing paradigm.

The future customer success organization will mainly comprise three key profiles, the most crucial being the account management roles. Account Managers function as farmer-hunters, skilled at cultivating long-lasting relationships with customers. They ensure customers consistently extract value from the platform, stay actively involved and committed, and expand their platform usage. These roles will be linked to revenue targets. A CSM looking to transition into this role must refine skills in value selling, cold calling, and executive engagement.

Another role I anticipate within Customer Success organizations is that of operational management. As emphasized, digital customer success teams are poised to become indispensable for organizations seeking efficient engagement with their long-tail customers, particularly those with lower revenue or less demand for continuous attention from full-scale CSMs. Consequently, traditional CSM roles may be replaced by digital CSMs, who will engage with customers as needed and function as pooled resources. These professionals will handle customer inquiries regarding product adoption, usage, or value as they arise. Typically, they excel as problem solvers with less experience than other roles discussed. To advance into leadership positions within a digital CSM team, individuals should prioritize refining skills in strategic operations, data analysis, and people management.

Within the domain of Customer Success, a third category of role will endure: that of industry experts or subject matter experts. These individuals boast extensive knowledge and insight into specific industry segments or platforms. B2B SaaS companies will deploy these experts to address customer challenges and assist large enterprises in navigating short-term hurdles. Customers willingly invest in these roles due to their broad experience across multiple industry segments, empowering executives to make well-informed decisions. Consequently, these resources are regarded as profit centers, with customers valuing their expertise in thought leadership and innovation.

Furthermore, these experts excel at tackling specific issues, leveraging their wealth of experience to help customers overcome temporary obstacles. Aspiring leaders in the industry can develop their expertise by joining subject matter groups, subscribing to industry-specific content, or pursuing further education in their chosen field. These evolving roles undergo continual refinement and adaptation, mirroring the dynamic nature of the Customer Success landscape.

In conclusion, the landscape of B2B SaaS is rapidly evolving, demanding that Customer Success Managers (CSMs) remain vigilant amidst market trends and profitability considerations. Traditional CSM roles give way to digital CSMs, who engage with customers as needed, while product teams take on a larger role in driving platform adoption. Automation and scalable communication are essential for optimizing platform usage. Account management and operational roles are pivotal within customer success organizations, with a growing emphasis on digital teams. Moreover, subject matter experts are increasingly valuable for addressing customer challenges and guiding decision-making. Adaptability and ongoing skill development are paramount for success in this dynamic environment.

ABOUT THE AUTHOR

With a rich and extensive background in customer success spanning across diverse industries and various customer success (CS) functions, Atma Gunupudi has undoubtedly made a lasting imprint on the field. Throughout his career, Atma has dedicated a significant portion of his professional journey to mastering the intricacies of customer success discipline, earning him high praise for his deep expertise in the domain.

Currently serving as the leader of all post-sales customer-facing teams at MoEngage, Atma showcases his adeptness in managing an impressive portfolio comprising thousands of eclectic customers. His strategic initiatives and adept leadership have consistently driven substantial revenue, amounting to over a hundred million throughout his career trajectory. Atma's ability to navigate complex customer landscapes and deliver tangible results underscores his exceptional talent in the realm of customer success.

Furthermore, Atma's influence transcends geographical boundaries, as evidenced by his track record of providing invaluable counsel to numerous CXOs and CS heads across different countries. His insights and guidance have been instrumental in both establishing and fortifying robust customer success functions, contributing to organizational growth and sustainability on a global scale.

www.ingramcontent.com/pod-product-compliance
Lightning Source LLC
Chambersburg PA
CBHW032358040426
42451CB00006B/52